Encyclopedia

A DORLING KINDERSLEY BOOK

DK

LONDON, NEW YORK, TORONTO, MELBOURNE,
MUNICH, and DELHI

Authors Anita Ganeri and Chris Oxlade
Project editor Simon Holland
Senior art editor Tory Gordon-Harris
Editor Sue Malyan
Art editor Rebecca Johns
Managing editors Mary Ling, Sue Leonard
Managing art editors Rachael Foster,
Cathy Chesson
Jacket design Sophia Tampakopoulos
Picture researcher Brenda Clynch
Production controller Jenny Jacoby
DTP designer Almudena Díaz

First published in hardback in Great Britain in 2002 by
Dorling Kindersley Limited
80 Strand, London WC2R 0RL

A Penguin Company

This paperback edition published in 2003

4 6 8 10 9 7 5 3

Copyright © 2002, © 2003 Dorling Kindersley Limited, London

A CIP catalogue record for this book
is available from the British Library.

ISBN-13: 978-1-4053-0155-8
Colour reproduction by Colourscan, Singapore
Printed and bound in China by SNP Leefung

see our complete
catalogue at
www.dk.com

Contents

World Regions

People and Society

History of People

Living World

This book will ask you lots of tricky questions...

Space and the Universe

Reference Section

Science and Technology

Planet Earth

About this book

The pages of this book have special features that will show you how to get your hands on as much information as possible! Look out for these:

The Curiosity Quiz will get you searching through each chapter for the answers.

Page references tell you where to look for more information on a subject.

Every page is colour coded to show you which chapter it is in.

get Mucky Activities show you how you can try things out for yourself.

World Map

A world map, like the one below, shows what the world looks like if it is stretched out. Before maps like this could be made, people had to travel far and wide around the world.

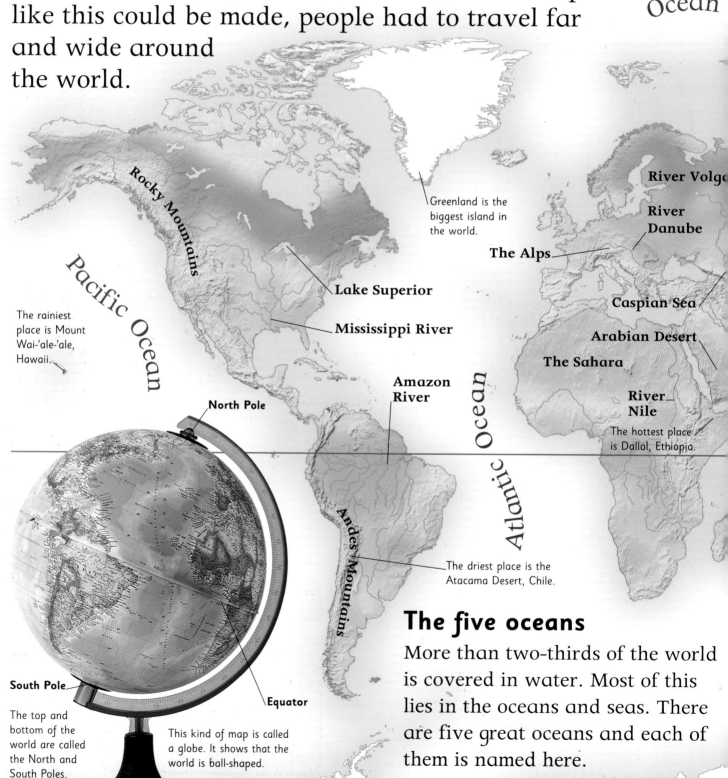

Arctic Ocean

Rocky Mountains

Pacific Ocean

Greenland is the biggest island in the world.

River Volga

River Danube

The Alps

Lake Superior

The rainiest place is Mount Wai-'ale-'ale, Hawaii.

Caspian Sea

Arabian Desert

Mississippi River

The Sahara

Amazon River

River Nile

The hottest place is Dallol, Ethiopia.

North Pole

Atlantic Ocean

Andes Mountains

The driest place is the Atacama Desert, Chile.

The five oceans

More than two-thirds of the world is covered in water. Most of this lies in the oceans and seas. There are five great oceans and each of them is named here.

South Pole

Equator

The top and bottom of the world are called the North and South Poles.

This kind of map is called a globe. It shows that the world is ball-shaped.

Antarctica

4

What is the Equator?

Physical features

This map shows the world's physical features. This means places like mountains, deserts, and lakes. Can you find the longest river on Earth?

 Mount Everest, in the Himalaya Mountains, Asia, is the highest mountain.

 The River Nile is the world's longest river. It snakes through Africa.

 The Pacific Ocean is the largest ocean. It covers about a third of the Earth.

Ural Mountains

Lake Baikal

Gobi Desert

Himalaya Mountains

Mount Everest

Yangtze River

 **The Sahara**, in the northern part of Africa, is the world's biggest desert.

Lake Superior is the largest lake. It is one of North America's five "Great Lakes".

The Equator

Indian Ocean

Great Sandy Desert

Great Victoria Desert

The windiest place is Commonwealth Bay, Antarctica.

Southern Ocean

The coldest place is the Pole of Inaccessibility, Antarctica.

Curiosity quiz

Look through the World Regions pages and see if you can identify each of the picture clues below.

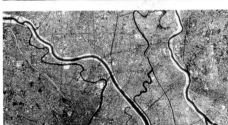
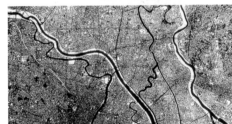

Turn and learn

24-25 World of People
64-65 World of Life
124-125 Our Planet

It is an imaginary line around the middle of the Earth.

Countries and Continents

The world is divided into more than 190 countries in seven continents. Each country usually has its own leaders and makes it own laws.

North America is made up of Canada, the USA, and Mexico. The USA is divided into 50 states.

The world's seven continents

North America

South America

Ancient continents

Millions of years ago, the continents were joined together with a huge sea around them. Slowly, they split up and moved apart.

The continents 200 million years ago

The continents 135 million years ago

The continents 10 million years ago

Rivers, mountains, and seas make natural borders between countries.

Caracas

Venezuela

Bogotá

Colombia

Quito

Equador

Peru

Lima

Georgetown

Paramaribo

Cayenne

Guyana

Surinam

French Guiana

São Paulo, in Brazil, is the world's fourth largest city. It has 18 million people.

Brazil

La Paz

Bolivia

Sucre

Brasilia

São Paulo

Paraguay

Asunción

Countries

On this map, you can see the different countries in the continent of South America. Some countries are tiny. Others, such as Brazil, are huge.

Chile

Santiago

Uruguay

Buenos Aires

Montevideo

Argentina

Capital cities

A country's most important city is called the capital. This is where the country's government meets and makes laws. Buenos Aires is the capital of Argentina.

Buenos Aires

These islands are called the Falkland Islands.

South America is the fourth largest continent.

Which country has the most neighbours?

The continents today

You can see the position of today's seven continents on the map below. Can you find the continent that your home country is in?

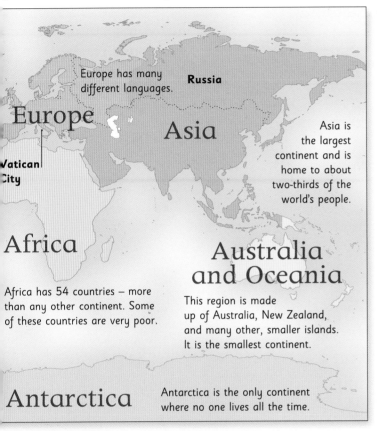

Europe has many different languages.

Europe

Russia

Asia

Asia is the largest continent and is home to about two-thirds of the world's people.

Vatican City

Africa

Africa has 54 countries – more than any other continent. Some of these countries are very poor.

Australia and Oceania

This region is made up of Australia, New Zealand, and many other, smaller islands. It is the smallest continent.

Antarctica

Antarctica is the only continent where no one lives all the time.

Saint Basil's Cathedral, Moscow

The biggest country

Russia is the biggest country in the world. It covers more than 17 million square km (6.8 million square miles) and stretches across both Europe and Asia.

Moscow is the capital of Russia.

The smallest country

The Vatican City in Rome, Italy, is the smallest country. Only about 1,000 people live in the Vatican City.

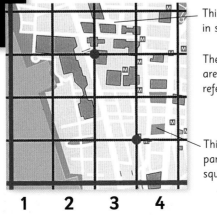

a

Making maps

Maps used to be drawn by hand. Today, planes and satellites take pictures of the landscape. These are fed into computers, which turn them into maps.

This street is in square 3a.

These codes are called grid references.

This public park is in square 4c.

Using a grid

Some maps have a grid plan, which helps you to find out where a place is. On this map, each square has its own letter and number.

b

c

d

1 2 3 4

get into it

Maps of the countries and continents are grouped together in books called atlases. See if you can find an atlas and use it to find your home country.

China – it has 16 countries around it.

Seas and Oceans

About two-thirds of the Earth is covered in salty sea. This lies in five oceans – the Pacific, Atlantic, Indian, Southern, and Arctic. These oceans all flow into each other.

Volcanoes and islands

Under the sea, there are mountains, valleys, plains, and volcanoes, just as there are on land. Some volcanoes are so tall that their tops poke out of the water and form islands.

Flippers help divers to swim underwater.

Why the sea is salty
Sea water tastes salty because it has got salt, and other minerals, dissolved in it. This is the same type of salt that you sprinkle on your food. The salt mostly washes into the sea from the land.

Many coral reef fish have colours that help them to blend in and hide from predators, or to look dangerous – as a warning to predators.

Become an expert

Life in the sea
Coral reefs are like beautiful gardens under the sea. Coral is made of the skeletons of millions of tiny sea animals. Thousands of sharks, fish, and other creatures live on coral reefs.

Which is the biggest coral reef in the world?

Oceans in motion

The water in the oceans is always moving. Great bands of water, called currents, flow like rivers in the sea and the wind blows the water into waves. Every day, the ocean tides rise and fall.

Frozen ocean

The Arctic Ocean is the world's smallest ocean. It is also the coldest. For most of the year, it is frozen over. This means that the North Pole is in the middle of a huge area of floating ice.

Special ships called ice-breakers can cut a path through the floating ice.

Black tip reef shark

Coral

The Great Barrier Reef, off the north-east coast of Australia.

Deserts

Deserts are the driest places on Earth. Sometimes no rain falls in the desert for years and years. By day, deserts may be baking hot, but at night they can be freezing cold.

A long line of camels, called a caravan, crossing the Takla Makan Desert in China

Desert animals

Animals that live in the desert have special ways of staying cool and finding water. Camels can go for days without food or water. This makes them very useful for desert transport.

Sand dunes can gradually creep forwards

Sand is made from tiny fragments of rock.

This is a Saguaro cactus.

Desert plants

Desert plants, such as this giant cactus, store water in their thick stems. Cacti are covered with sharp spines to stop hungry creatures eating them. Cacti grow in the American deserts.

Sandy deserts

Some deserts, such as the Namib Desert in Africa, are covered in vast seas of sand. The wind blows the sand into huge piles, called sand dunes. Some dunes can be 200 m (650 ft) high.

Which is the world's largest desert?

Rocky deserts

These deserts are made of rocky plains covered in pebbles and gravel. The wind blows sand against the rocks, carving them into fantastic shapes.

These desert mountains have been shaped by wind-blown sand.

These flat-topped rock formations are called buttes. These buttes, in Monument Valley, USA, have been named "Mitten Rocks".

Desert people

Some desert people are nomads. Nomads wander from place to place looking for food and water. They live in tents, which are easy to move.

...and sometimes bury

whole villages under sand.

Water in the desert

In some places, water from deep underground seeps up to the surface. This is called an oasis. Here trees and plants can grow, and people can find drinking water.

The Sahara in Africa.

11

Grasslands

Grasslands are dusty plains that are too dry for many plants to grow. There are grasslands in many parts of the world.

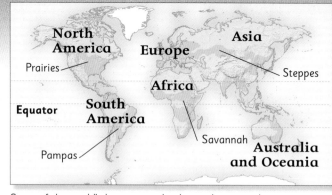

Some of the world's largest grasslands are shown on this map.

Grassland trees

Few trees grow in grasslands because the soil is too sandy and dry. Baobab trees survive by storing water in their huge trunks. The trunks shrink as the water is used up.

African grasslands

Many different animals live in grasslands, where they graze on the grass. In an African grassland, large herds of zebras roam the plains, together with impalas, wildebeest, elephants, and giraffes.

Become an expert

68-69 Trees and Forests

74-75 Mammals

136-137 Weather

Grassland animals travel long distances to drink at a waterhole.

How many different types of grass are there?

The prairies

In North America, grasslands are called prairies. Large parts of the prairies have been turned into fields where farmers grow wheat and other crops.

Huge areas of pampas are covered in spiky pampas grass.

Harvesting wheat on an American prairie field

The pampas

The grasslands of South America are called pampas. They are home to some unusual animals, such as giant anteaters, vizcachas (burrowing rodents), and rheas (flightless birds).

Animal scavengers

Some grassland animals, such as vultures, are scavengers. They soar above the ground looking for a dead animal. Then they swoop down to feed on the scraps.

A white-backed vulture on the lookout for food

Tough plants, such as grasses and thorny trees, can grow in the grasslands.

Impalas are hunted by animals such as cheetahs and jackals.

Rainforests

Rainforests are hot, steamy jungles that grow near the Equator. They are home to more than half of all the types of plants and animals on Earth.

Rainforests are hot and steamy because they grow mainly in the warm areas near the Equator, called the tropics.

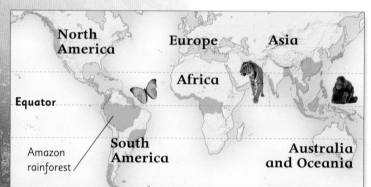

North America

Europe

Asia

Africa

Equator

Amazon rainforest

South America

Australia and Oceania

The world's biggest rainforests are shown in green on this map.

Rainforests cover a small part of the Earth but contain thousands of plants and animals.

Forest layers

Rainforest trees grow in layers. Each layer has its own plants, insects, birds, and animals.

 The emergent layer has the tallest trees. Their tops tower above the ground.

 The canopy is like a thick, green umbrella. Most animals live here.

 The understorey has shorter trees, covered in creepers and vines.

 The forest floor is gloomy, dark, and covered in dead leaves, fungi, and ferns.

Animals

Every part of the rainforest is alive with animals, from spectacular butterflies to parrots, frogs, snakes, jaguars, and millions of creepy-crawlies.

Which are the most dangerous ants of all?

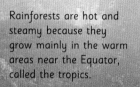

Rainforest riches

Food, wood, medicines, and other useful products come from rainforest plants. Even chocolate comes from the beans of a rainforest tree.

Doctors use this plant to treat leukaemia, a blood disease.

Rosy periwinkle

Biggest rainforest

The world's biggest rainforest grows along the banks of the Amazon River in South America. The forest is about the same size as Australia.

Hot and wet

In the rainforest, the weather is hot and wet all year round. Animals, such as this orang-utan, use an umbrella of leaves to shelter from the pouring rain.

Some orchids dangle their roots in the air to soak up water.

Plants

The steamy rainforest heat is ideal for many plants to bloom. Some plants, such as these beautiful orchids, grow high up on the branches of the canopy trees.

Become an expert

Army ants. They attack and kill animals.

Rivers and Lakes

Many rivers start as a stream or spring, high up on a mountainside. As the water flows downhill, other streams flow into it to make a river.

Waterfalls

When a river flows over bands of soft and hard rock, it wears the soft rock away. This leaves a step of hard rock, which the river plunges over. This makes a waterfall.

Stages of a river

At first, a river flows very fast. It slows down as it reaches flat land, where it drops sand and mud that it has carried from the hills. Finally, the river flows into the sea.

A steamboat on the Mississippi River in the USA

River transport

For thousands of years, people have used rivers to carry people, animals, and goods. Barges, steamboats, and canoes are different types of river transport.

Which is the world's longest river?

River life

Many amazing animals are suited to life in or near the world's rivers.

Piranhas are ferocious fish with razor-sharp teeth for snapping up their prey.

Otters are rare animals with sleek, streamlined bodies for swimming.

Crocodiles hide in the water, then leap out to grab their prey.

Water boatmen are insects that use their legs to row across the water.

Salty lakes

Some lakes are filled with salty water. The Dead Sea, between Israel and Jordan, is so salty that you can float in it and read a newspaper!

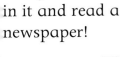

This lake is called the Dead Sea because no fish can live there.

Become an expert

Lesser flamingoes

Lakes

A lake is a large stretch of water surrounded by land. It is made when rain or river water fills a large hollow or dip in the ground.

Many lakes form high up in the mountains, where ice has carved out a hollow.

Largest lakes

The world's biggest freshwater lake is Lake Superior in the USA and Canada. It is part of a group of five huge lakes, called the Great Lakes.

Flamingoes get their pink colour from the food they eat.

Flamingoes use their curved beaks to sieve lake water for food.

Lake life

Lakes are home to hundreds of plants and animals. Huge flocks of brightly coloured flamingoes build their nests on the shores of some lakes in Africa.

The River Nile in Africa.

Mountains

When two huge chunks of the Earth's rocky crust crash or push into each other, a mighty mountain is made.

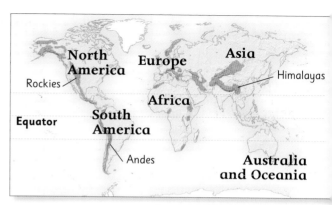

Some of the world's biggest mountain ranges are shown in brown on this map

The high life

High up on a mountainside, it is cold and windy. The air is thin and hard to breathe. Despite this, many people live in the mountains. These people come from Tibet in Asia.

Mount Everest

Most of the world's highest mountain peaks are in Asia. Everest, in the Himalayas, is the highest mountain on Earth. It is 8,850 m (29,035 ft) tall.

The Himalayas are the world's highest mountain range.

Mount Everest

18

What does the name "Himalaya" mean?

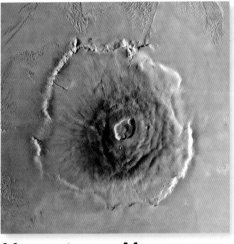

Mountain animals

Despite the extreme weather, many animals live in the mountains.

Snow leopards from the Himalayas have thick fur coats to keep them warm.

Spectacled bears from the Andes eat leaves, fruit, eggs, and small mammals.

Mountain gorillas from Africa have been hunted and are very rare.

Golden eagles soar high above the mountain peaks of Europe.

Mountain lions are fast, clever hunters from North and South America.

Mountains on Mars

Did you know that there are mountains on other planets? This is Olympus Mons on Mars. It is a gigantic volcano, three times higher than Mount Everest. The crater on top is the size of two large cities.

Mountain danger

Sometimes huge amounts of ice and snow break loose and crash down a mountainside. This is called an avalanche. The snow can bury people, and even whole villages, in its path.

This strong rope would hold the climber if he fell.

The climber's boots help him to grip the rock.

Mountain sports

Many people enjoy walking, climbing, and skiing in the mountains. Some mountain sports can be dangerous, so people use special safety equipment.

Home of the snows.

Polar regions

The Poles are at the top and bottom of the Earth. They are the coldest places on the planet, with ice as far as the eye can see.

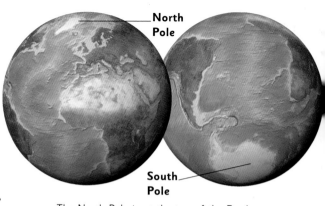

The North Pole is at the top of the Earth. The South Pole is at the bottom.

The Arctic

The Arctic is the region around the North Pole. The Pole lies in the middle of the icy Arctic Ocean, which freezes over for most of the year.

Polar bears can travel long distances using huge pieces of ice as rafts.

Life on the tundra

The tundra is a vast, icy area around the Arctic. It is frozen in winter but thaws out in summer. Caribou (reindeer) graze on the tundra plants.

Arctic people

People have lived in the Arctic for thousands of years. They are experts at surviving in the cold. These Inuit children are dressed in their warm, winter clothes.

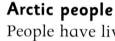

Inuit people sometimes use skidoos (sledges with motors) to race across the icy ground.

Apart from Antarctica, where else do penguins live?

Antarctica

The region around the South Pole is called Antarctica. Antarctica is a large piece of land covered in a thick sheet of ice. Antarctica is one of the seven continents, and is bigger than Europe.

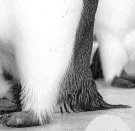

Halley Station, Antarctica

Antarctic science

Despite the cold conditions, thousands of scientists work in Antarctica. They spend their time studying the ice, the wildlife, and the weather. They live at research stations like this one.

Antarctic mountains

Antarctic wildlife

Some amazing animals live in Antarctica. Emperor penguins have thick, waterproof and windproof feathers, with a layer of fat underneath. This keeps them warm and dry in the freezing temperatures.

Emperor penguin chicks are born in the middle of winter.

The coasts of South America, Africa, Australia, New Zealand, and the Galápagos Islands.

The Empire State Building is New York's most famous skyscraper.

Great cities

Millions of people live and work in the world's cities. People also visit cities to go shopping, or to see the sights.

Rio de Janeiro

Rio is the second-biggest city in Brazil. It is surrounded by steep hills and beautiful beaches. There are stylish apartment blocks, but many poor people live in Rio's "shanty towns" (slums).

The Empire State Building

The Eiffel Tower

Paris

The beautiful city of Paris is the capital of France. The city's most famous landmark is the Eiffel Tower. Paris has many fine clothes shops, restaurants, and street cafés.

The Tower of London

You can see the whole of Paris from any of the Eiffel Tower's three viewing floors.

London

London is the capital city of England and the United Kingdom. It is one of the world's most important business centres. London has many famous palaces, churches, and bridges.

New York

New York is the largest city in the USA. This city is famous for its skyscrapers and yellow taxis. People from all over the world live in New York.

Which great city is the capital of Russia?

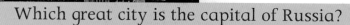

Capital cities

A country's capital is the city where its government meets. Here are some record-breaking capital cities.

 Tokyo, in Japan, is the biggest capital with more than 27 million people.

 Damascus, Syria, is the oldest capital. People have lived there for 2,500 years.

 Lhasa, in Tibet, is the world's highest capital at 3,684 m (12,087 ft).

 Reykjavik, in Iceland, is the world's most northerly capital city.

 Wellington, in New Zealand, is the world's most southerly capital.

Shanghai

Shanghai is one of the biggest cities in China. The old part of the city has narrow, crowded streets. Shanghai is one of the world's largest ports and has factories that make steel and ships.

Cairo

Cairo is the capital of Egypt. Cairo's old streets are full of markets called bazaars. The ancient pyramids stand in the desert on the edge of the modern city.

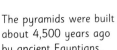

The pyramids were built about 4,500 years ago by ancient Egyptians.

Sydney harbour

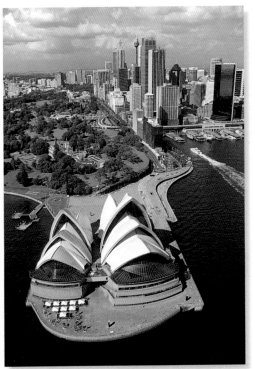

Sydney

Sydney is Australia's largest and oldest city. The Sydney Opera House looks over the city's harbour, where there is a huge port. The Olympic Games were held in Sydney in 2000.

Become an expert

World of People

More than six billion people live in the world. These people have different customs, languages, beliefs, and lifestyles.

Language and people

One in every five people in the world lives in China. The most widely spoken language is Mandarin Chinese, which has almost one billion speakers.

This girl is dressed up for May Day – a festival that is celebrated in some parts of Europe.

Culture

People enjoy many different kinds of art and culture.

Writing is used to record information, news, views, stories, and history.

Theatre entertains audiences with acting, dance, and costume.

Painting is a way of expressing feelings and ideas through pictures.

May Day marks the first day of spring, after the long, cold months of winter.

Fashion is different all over the world, and is changing all the time.

Music styles can be classical or popular, traditional or modern.

Which is the second most spoken language?

At work

All over the world, people work to earn a living. What job would you like to do? You could be an astronaut or a teacher, a farmer or a computer programmer.

At play

Having time for leisure and play is very important. Some people like watching or playing sport. Like these children, you might enjoy playing games with friends.

Celebrations

Important times in people's lives are celebrated with special feasts and festivals. These are times for people to enjoy themselves and to share their religious beliefs.

At some festivals in India, people exchange gifts of sweets, like these.

Curiosity quiz

Look through the People and Society pages and see if you can identify the picture clues below.

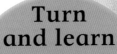

Turn and learn

Religious lands

Many people follow a religion. A religion is a set of beliefs and a way of worship. The main religions today are Hinduism, Judaism, Buddhism, Christianity, Islam, and Sikhism.

Hinduism

Hinduism began in India about 4,000 years ago. Hindus believe in a spirit called Brahman (God). They also worship many gods and goddesses, who represent different parts of Brahman.

Hindus bathing in the holy River Ganges, in India

The Church of the Holy Sepulchre, in Jerusalem

Rosary

Sacred symbols

Each of these symbols has a special meaning.

Hinduism: the "Aum" symbol represents the first sound of creation.

Judaism: the Star of David reminds Jews of a great Jewish king.

Buddhism: the wheel represents eight points of the Buddha's teaching.

Christianity: the cross reminds Christians of Jesus' death on a cross.

Islam: the star and crescent moon appear on many Islamic flags.

Sikhism: the khanda symbol reminds Sikhs of God and of God's power

Christianity

Christians follow the teachings of a man called Jesus Christ who lived about 2,000 years ago. They believe that Jesus was the son of God, who died to save them from sin.

What is the Christian holy book called?

This building is a Buddhist monastery in Thailand.

Islam

People who follow Islam are called Muslims. They believe in Allah (God), who guides them through their lives. The holy book of Islam is called the Qur'an (Koran). It contains the teachings of a prophet called Mohammed.

Mecca (Makkah) is a holy city for Muslims.

Western Wall

The Western Wall (Wailing Wall), in Jerusalem, is a holy place for Jews.

Buddhism

Buddhists follow the teachings of the Buddha. He was an Indian prince who lived about 2,500 years ago. He showed people how to live good, happy lives, full of peace.

Statues of the Buddha often show him meditating (thinking deeply).

Judaism

Judaism is the religion of the Jews. Their holy book is called the Torah. It tells the story of the Jewish people and their special relationship with God.

Menorah (Jewish candlestick)

Become an expert

The Golden Temple in Amritsar, India, is the holiest of all Sikh shrines.

Sikhism

The Sikh religion was started by a teacher called Guru Nanak. Sikhs worship in a building called a gurdwara. Their holy book is the Guru Granth Sahib.

The Bible.

Religious life

In their religious lives, people honour their God or gods. They may come together for worship and celebrate special events with feasts and festivals.

Statue of the Buddha

Islam

Muslims (followers of Islam) must pray five times a day: at dawn, midday, mid-afternoon, sunset, and night-time. Muslims follow a set of special prayer positions.

Buddhism

Buddhists do not worship a god, but honour the life and teachings of the Buddha. In the temple, they offer flowers, candles, and incense to the Buddha, to show their respect.

In some Buddhist countries, boys spend time as monks.

What is a mosque?

In a synagogue, Jews listen to readings from the Torah, their holy book.

Torah scroll

Silver pointer

Judaism

Jewish people meet to worship and pray in a special building called a synagogue. A man or woman called a rabbi leads the worship.

Turban

Small sword

Steel bangle

Sikhism

Many Sikh men wear five things to show their faith. These are uncut hair (often kept tidy in a turban), a wooden comb, a small sword, a steel bangle, and white undershorts.

This is Ganesha, the elephant-headed god.

Hinduism

Hindus worship the gods and goddesses in their homes and in mandirs (temples). The god Ganesha is said to bring good luck and success.

Christianity

Christmas is a joyful festival when Christians remember how Jesus was born. There are services in church, and people celebrate by exchanging cards and gifts.

Jesus was born in a stable in Bethlehem. Three kings brought presents for him.

These children are acting out the story of the first Christmas.

Joseph

Three kings

Jesus

Mary

A building where Muslims worship Allah (God).

Writing and Printing

People began to write things down about 5,500 years ago. Before this, they told stories and passed news on by word of mouth. Today, writing is all around you.

The alphabet

Fountain pens are filled with ink.

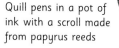

Quill pens in a pot of ink with a scroll made from papyrus reeds

Paper and pens

The paper you use today comes from trees. Long ago, people made paper from reeds or animal skins. The first pens were pieces of reeds, dipped in soot or ink.

Signs and symbols

Sometimes, signs and symbols are used to write letters and words, or even secret codes.

Pictograms are pictures used for writing. This old, Chinese word means "to sell".

Hieroglyphs were used by the ancient Egyptians. This one stands for "chick".

Runes were Viking symbols that were carved on stone or wood. This is the "M" sound.

Music symbols like these are used to write down musical sounds (notes).

Morse code changes the alphabet into dot and dash signals for sending messages.

Writing machines

The first typewriters were invented about 200 years ago. They made writing much quicker. Today, modern word processors, like this lap-top computer, are used instead.

Early typewriter

Lap-top computer

How long did it take to create this book?

Printing books

At first, books were written out by hand. This took a long time and was very costly. Printing presses, like the one shown here, were first used about 600 years ago. Printing books by machine was much quicker and cheaper.

An old wooden printing press

The different parts of the machine were worked by hand.

Become an expert

48-49 Ancient Egypt
54-55 The Vikings
118-119 Machines and Computers

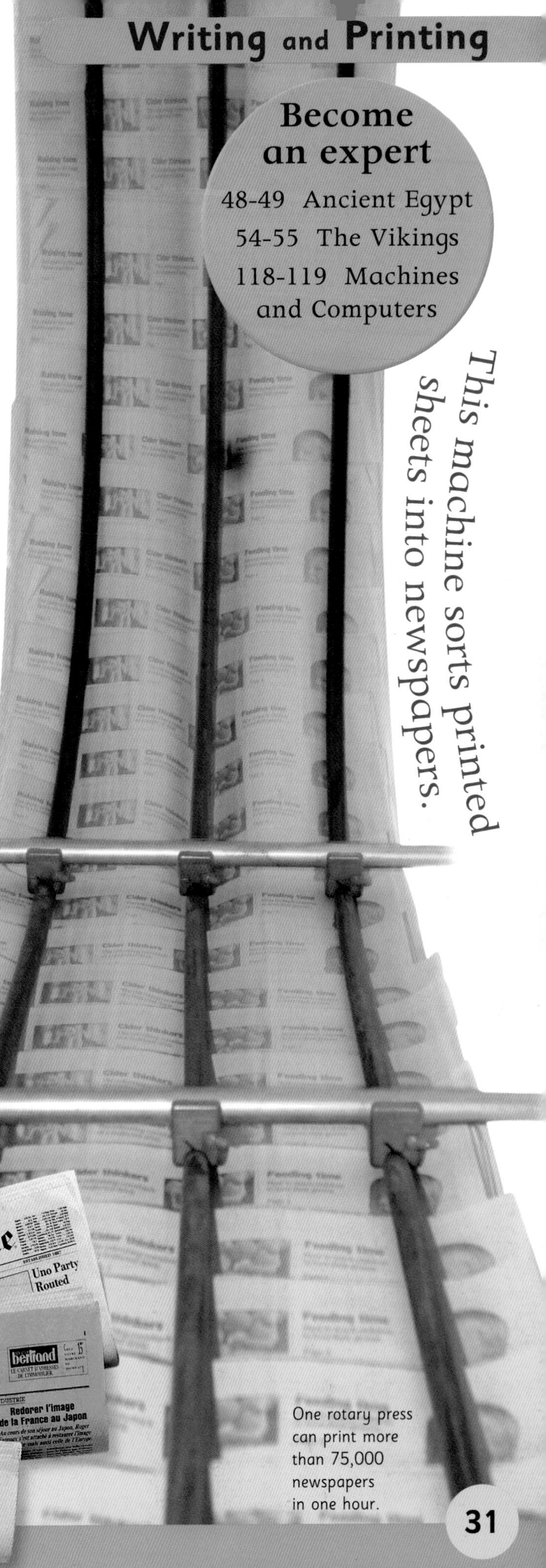

This machine sorts printed sheets into newspapers.

Printing the news

The first, hand-written newspapers date from Roman times. They told people about battles and gladiator contests. Today, giant rotary presses are used to print millions of books, newspapers, and magazines every day.

Every day, newspapers tell us what is happening in the world.

One rotary press can print more than 75,000 newspapers in one hour.

About one year.

Art and Architecture

Since ancient times, artists have painted pictures and used stone and wood to make sculptures. Architects plan the world's buildings.

Cave painting
Prehistoric artists painted pictures of figures and animals on cave walls. This cave art is from the USA.

Church art
The Italian artist Michelangelo painted scenes from the Bible on the ceiling and walls of the Sistine Chapel in Rome, Italy.

Modern sculpture
Modern British artist Henry Moore used bold shapes to create this interesting – and "touchable" – giant stone sculpture.

Architecture can change the way a whole city looks.

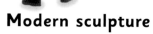
Skyscraper

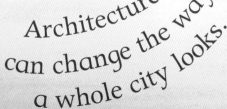

Singapore skyline

Which is the world's tallest building?

Architecture

Every building you see has been planned by an architect. Styles of architecture have changed over thousands of years. Buildings are designed for living, working, worship, or simply for fun.

Castles were built to defend people from attack. This castle is in Spain.

The Taj Mahal

The beautiful Taj Mahal in India was built as a tomb for the emperor's wife. It is made from white marble set with coloured stones.

Modern skyscrapers make up the Singapore skyline.

Making art

People use different types of art to capture a scene or express their ideas. Here are a few of them.

Drawing a quick "sketch" in pencil is a way for artists to plan a colour painting.

Painting in colour is often done on a canvas using watercolour or oil paints.

Sculpture is the skill of making artistic shapes out of stone, wood, or metal.

Photography is a very accurate way of showing how people and places look.

Graphic design is how artists play with colours and designs on a computer.

An opera house

The Opera House in Sydney, Australia, is a modern building. Its wing-like roof makes it easy to identify. It was designed to look like the sails of boats in the nearby harbour.

Become an expert

The Petronas Towers in Malaysia. They are 452 m (1,483 ft) tall.

Music

What is your favourite song o
tune? Do you like classical, ja:
folk, rock, or pop music? If yo
play a musical instrument, yo
can make music of your own.

Conductor

An orchestra

Some musicians perform together
in a group called an orchestra.
There are about 90 musicians in a
symphony orchestra. The conducto
keeps them in time. Orchestras
usually play classical music.

Drums and cymbals are
percussion instruments.

Cymbal

Drum

Musical instruments

In an orchestra, there are
four kinds of instruments —
brass, woodwind, percussion,
and strings. Each instrument
makes its own individual
sound. The different sounds
blend together.

Flute

What sort of instrument is a xylophone?

Recording music

In a recording studio, each voice or instrument can be recorded on its own. These are called tracks. Engineers mix the tracks together.

Mixing desk

The knobs on the mixing desk control the volume and tone of each track.

Types of music

Many different kinds of music are played all over the world.

Early music was probably played on instruments made from animal bones.

Opera is a play set to music in which the performers sing their lines.

Jazz musicians make up some or all of the music as they play it.

Rock music, or rock and roll, has punchy lyrics (words) and a strong beat.

Pop is short for popular music. It has catchy tunes and is good for dancing to.

Madonna is one of the most successful pop singers of all time.

Madonna

Vinyl record

CDs

Minidisc   **Tape**

You can listen to music on vinyl records, tapes, CDs, minidiscs, or on a computer.

Many rock and pop musicians play music on electric guitars.

Pop concerts

Watching your favourite pop star perform live on stage can be thrilling. Many people work behind the scenes to make the show run smoothly.

Cello

French horn

Piano keyboard

A percussion instrument.

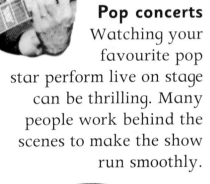

get into it

Would you like to be a pop star? Try writing your own pop song. Start by writing a poem, then make up a tune to go with it.

Theatre and Dance

Theatre began thousands of years ago in ancient Greece. Actors and dancers put on shows to entertain and inform people.

Actors and acting

Putting on a play is a long task. First, the playwright writes the play. Then actors bring the story and the characters in the play to life. They also have to remember their words!

Actors use their body, as well as the words, to create a character and perform the scenes.

These actors are playing two characters, called Romeo and Juliet.

Costumes help to show when and where the play's action is happening.

Musical theatre

Going to the theatre to see a musical is a special treat. Musicals are an exciting mixture of acting, dancing, and song. This is a scene from the musical "Oliver!"

Who wrote the play "Romeo and Juliet"?

Japanese theatre

These actors are performing an ancient type of Japanese play, called Kabuki. They wear beautiful costumes and mix acting, singing, dancing, and music to put on a dazzling show.

Forms of dance

There are many different types and styles of dance from all over the world.

Tap dancers wear metal-capped shoes to make "tap" sounds.

Ballet is a graceful type of dance, set to music, that tells a tale.

Country and **folk** dances from around the world are lively and fun.

Flamenco is a dramatic Spanish dance set to the sound of clicking castanets.

Jazz dance uses the rhythm and beat of jazz music to create an exciting dance.

Indian dance

Dancing is a way of telling a story or showing a feeling using movement and music. This type of dancing, from India, is made up of special movements and expressions.

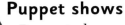

Puppet shows

Puppet shows are a very old type of theatre. These glove puppets are simple to work. A hand inside makes the puppet move. One finger works the puppet's head, while two other fingers work the arms.

Punch

Judy

Become an expert

Punch and Judy are famous puppets from Britain.

William Shakespeare.

Clothes and Fashion

What are you wearing today? A T-shirt? Trousers? Trainers? Clothes can make you look good. They may also have a special job to do.

Types of fabric

Cotton is made of fibres from the cotton plant. The fabric is usually woven.

Silk is a thin, soft fabric made from threads spun by silkworms.

Leather is made from the skins of animals such as cows.

Wool is made from the hair of sheep. It is often knitted to make clothes.

Nylon and other artificial fabrics are made from chemicals.

This Vietnamese boy is wearing casual clothes.

This Indian girl is wearing a sari.

A raincoat, Wellington boots, and umbrella are useful when it rains.

This French girl wears a top and skirt for school.

What do you wear?

What you wear depends on where you live and what you are doing. People wear different clothes for keeping warm, staying cool, for playing sport, and for going to school.

What is a beret ("berr-eh")?

Fashion shows
Some people design clothes to look stylish or unusual. They are called fashion designers. They put on fashion shows where models show off their clothes.

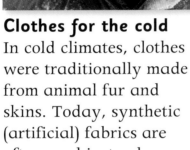

Clothes for the cold
In cold climates, clothes were traditionally made from animal fur and skins. Today, synthetic (artificial) fabrics are often used instead.

Uniforms
Some people have to wear special clothes for work. These are called uniforms. This fire-fighter's uniform protects against heat and flames. Do you wear a uniform at school?

This Masai girl from Tanzania is wearing her colourful national dress.

Children from the Arctic need thick, fur-lined clothes for warmth.

This beautiful outfit is the national dress of a hill tribe from Vietnam.

This girl is wearing a kimono, the national dress of Japan.

National dress
A country's traditional clothes are called its national dress. In many countries, people only wear their national dress for festivals or other special occasions.

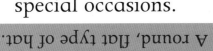
A round, flat type of hat.

39

Sport and Leisure

What do you do in your spare time? Do you enjoy a favourite sport? Or do you have fun with toys or play computer games?

Soccer is the most popular sport in the world.

Snowboarders wear warm, baggy clothes.

Plastic clips attach the boot to the snowboard.

Snowboarders do amazing spins and jumps.

Spectator sports

A spectator sport is a sport that people like to watch. Soccer, rugby, American football, baseball, and golf are all spectator sports.

Team sports

All of these spectator sports are played by two teams of players.

Baseball: teams score runs by batting. Fielders wear a catching glove.

Basketball: points are scored by throwing the ball into a raised hoop (basket)

Soccer: each team tries to kick or head the ball into the other team's net.

Ice hockey: teams score goals by hitting a puck with flat sticks.

Rugby: teams score "tries" by carrying the oval ball along the pitch.

Outdoor sports

Snowboarding, rock climbing, canoeing, skiing, and sailing are outdoor sports. You need special equipment and clothes to do outdoor sports safely.

Which games are played with cues on a table?

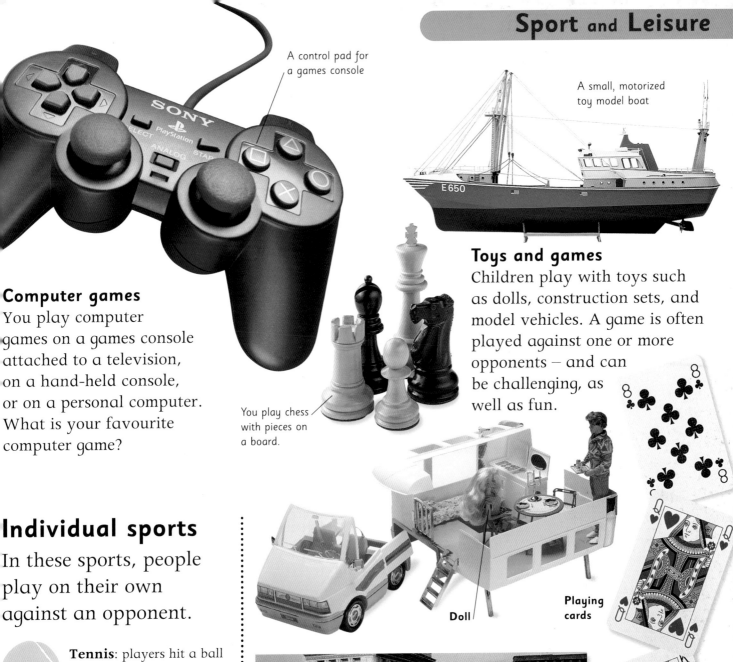

A control pad for a games console

A small, motorized toy model boat

E 650

Computer games

You play computer games on a games console attached to a television, on a hand-held console, or on a personal computer. What is your favourite computer game?

You play chess with pieces on a board.

Toys and games

Children play with toys such as dolls, construction sets, and model vehicles. A game is often played against one or more opponents – and can be challenging, as well as fun.

Doll

Playing cards

Individual sports

In these sports, people play on their own against an opponent.

Tennis: players hit a ball with rackets. They must keep the ball in the court.

Swimming: swimmers race each other up and down a pool.

Golf: players hit a ball around a course, using as few shots as they can.

Running: runners race against each other on a track or on roads.

Table tennis: players hit a ball with small bats. The game is played on a table.

Going to the movies

When new films are made, they are first shown on large screens at cinemas. Today, many films are made using animation and special effects.

Snooker, pool, and billiards.

Working people

What do you want to be when you grow up? All over the world, people do different kinds of work to earn the money to buy their food, clothes, and homes.

Astronauts

Astronauts are people who work in space. Some fly spacecraft. Others do science experiments in space. The astronauts in this picture are working inside a Space Shuttle.

Market sellers

There are markets selling food and other goods in almost every town and city. This man is selling fruit and vegetables from his market stall in Cairo, Egypt.

What do you call someone who writes books to earn a living?

This vet is giving a cat a health check.

The farmer's plough is being pulled by an ox.

Vets

If your pet is ill, you take it to the vet. Vets look after sick and injured animals. Some vets treat small animals, such as cats and dogs. Others work with farm or zoo animals.

Farmers

All over the world, farmers grow crops and raise animals. They grow food for themselves and to sell at market. This farmer is ploughing his rice field in Thailand.

Teachers

Who is your favourite teacher? At school, teachers help you to learn science, languages, and other subjects. Teachers have to go to college to learn how to teach you!

This teacher is helping some children to learn to read.

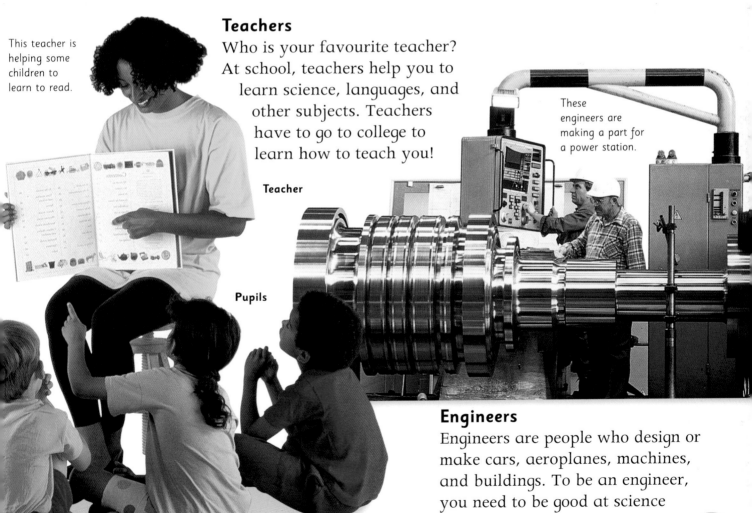

These engineers are making a part for a power station.

Teacher

Pupils

Engineers

Engineers are people who design or make cars, aeroplanes, machines, and buildings. To be an engineer, you need to be good at science and mathematics.

An author.

43

World of History

History tells us the story of how people lived in the past. From the things they left behind, we can find out about their homes, food, clothes, work, and beliefs.

The mummy mask of the Egyptian king, Tutankhamun

Decorative blue stones called lapis lazuli

Solid gold

Early people

About 10,000 years ago, groups of people began to settle down in certain places. They started to farm the land and to raise animals for food.

Early farmers cut down the ripe wheat stalks with a sickle made from a sharp flint stone set in a wooden handle.

People learnt how to grow crops for food.

Powerful kings

Many great civilizations were ruled by powerful kings. In ancient Egypt, the kings were called pharaohs. They were so important that people worshipped them as gods.

Spanish galleon

Where did the Aztecs and Incas live?

Greeks and Romans

About 2,500 years ago, ancient Greek culture flourished. Then the Romans grew in strength and ruled over a great empire from Rome in Italy.

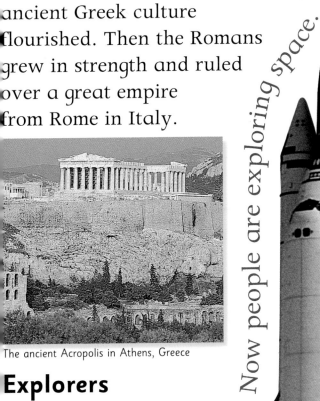

The ancient Acropolis in Athens, Greece

Explorers

For centuries, people have travelled far and wide across the world. They went in search of new lands, goods to trade, and adventures.

These coins were made by European explorers using the gold they discovered on their travels.

Now people are exploring space.

The first Space Shuttle flight was made in 1981 with a Shuttle called Columbia.

20th century

The 20th century saw many new inventions and discoveries being made. People flew in space for the first time, and even walked on the Moon.

Curiosity quiz

Look through the History of People pages and see if you can identify the picture clues below.

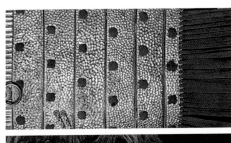

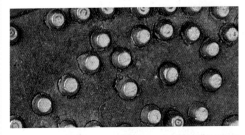

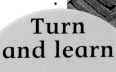

Turn and learn

30-31 Writing and Printing

60-61 Explorers

152-153 Space travel

In Central and South America.

Early people

The first human beings lived about two million years ago. We do not know exactly what they looked like, but we do know how they lived.

From apes to human beings

Our oldest ancestors looked like apes. Slowly, they became more human-like and began to walk upright on two legs.

Homo habilis skull

Neanderthal skull

Modern human skull

Cave shelters

Early people used caves like these as shelters. Inside, the caves were safe and warm. Sometimes, people painted the walls with pictures of the animals they hunted.

The first farmers

Until 10,000 years ago, people had to travel in search of food. Then they began to grow crops and keep animals for meat and milk. These people were the first farmers.

Fire

Flint blade

A flint hand axe from Egypt.

Tools and fire

We take fire and tools for granted, but early people had to learn how to make and use them. The first tools were stone hand axes, made about 600,000 years ago.

This woman is grinding grain between two stones to make flour for bread.

How did early people start fires?

The first cities
When people started growing their food, they were able to settle in one place. They began to build houses, villages, and cities. One of the first cities was Jericho in Jordan.

Early inventions
Here are some of the everyday things that early people used.

Dogs were first used for hunting about 10,000 years ago.

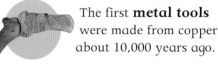
The first **metal tools** were made from copper about 10,000 years ago.

The first **clay pots** for storing water were made about 7,000 years ago.

Hunters and gatherers
Early people hunted woolly mammoths, cave bears, reindeer, and other animals for food. They also collected fruit, nuts, and roots, and caught fish.

Become an expert
22-23 Great cities

128-129 Rocks and Fossils

The meat from a mammoth was enough to feed a family for a whole year.

Hunters killed the mammoth with wooden spears.

Mammoth hunting was dangerous work!

47

By rubbing two sticks or striking two stones together.

Ancient Egypt

The ancient Egyptians lived by the banks of the River Nile about 3,500 years ago. Their powerful rulers were called pharaohs.

Beautifully decorated mummy

The pyramids

The ancient Egyptians believed in life after death. The pharaohs built magnificent tombs for themselves, called pyramids.

Mummy of a cat

Building skills

Egyptian builders did not have modern tools and machines to help them. The workers carried huge stone blocks into place, or sent them on barges along the river.

These men are carrying stone blocks for building, as the ancient Egyptians did.

Mummification

When an important person died, the body was "mummified". Some of the inside parts were removed. Then the body was treated with chemicals and wrapped in bandages.

get into it

Try writing out a message using only Egyptian hieroglyphics. You could also make up your own set of hieroglyphic symbols.

Why did the Egyptians mummify their dead?

The Nile floods

Each year, the River Nile flooded and spread rich, black soil on its banks. Farmers grew crops in the soil and used the river water to water their fields.

The River Nile Egypt

A funeral barge

Nile barges were important for transport.

Hieroglyphics

The Egyptians used picture writing called hieroglyphics. Symbols, such as those below, stood for letters and sounds.

Hieroglyphic sound chart

ah   b   c, k   d

ee, y   f   g   h

kh   m   n   p

r   s   t   oo, u, w

The Sphinx

A huge stone statue, called the Sphinx, guards the pyramids at Giza. It has the body of a lion and a human head, which was modelled on the pharaoh's own features.

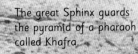

The mysterous Sphinx still stares out across the desert.

The great Sphinx guards the pyramid of a pharaoh called Khafra.

To keep the body whole for the next life.

Ancient Greece

About 2,500 years ago, Greece was made up of powerful "city-states", such as Athens and Sparta, that fought war against each other.

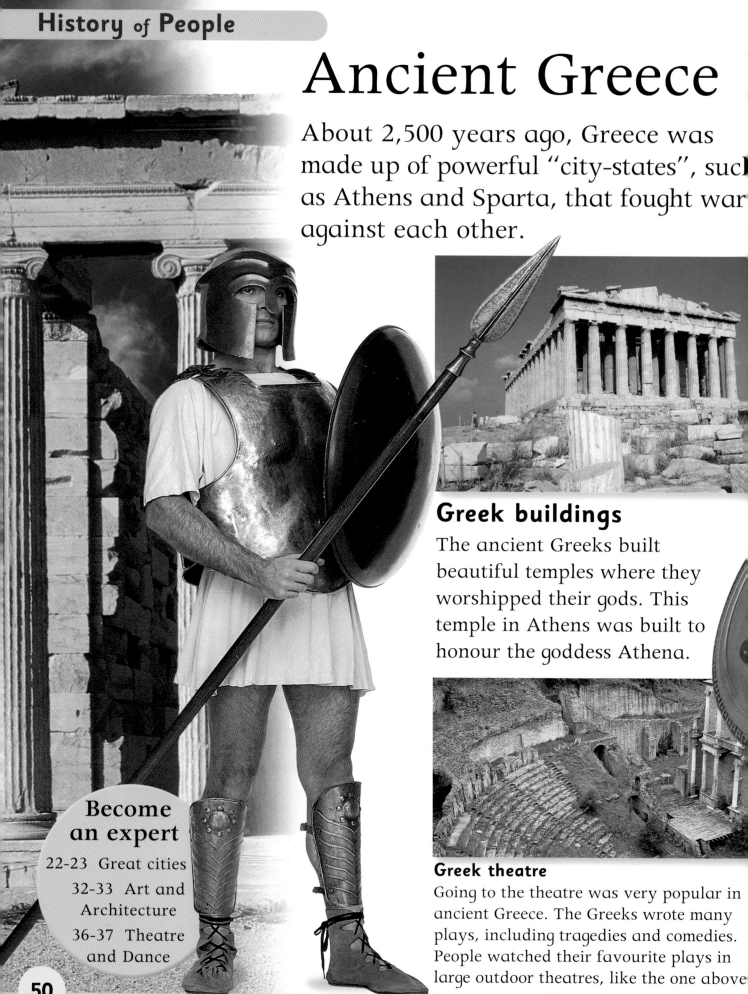

Greek buildings

The ancient Greeks built beautiful temples where they worshipped their gods. This temple in Athens was built to honour the goddess Athena.

Greek theatre

Going to the theatre was very popular in ancient Greece. The Greeks wrote many plays, including tragedies and comedies. People watched their favourite plays in large outdoor theatres, like the one above

Become an expert

Where were the first Olympic Games held?

The Trojan War

During a long war with the city of Troy, the Greeks gave the Trojans a huge wooden horse as a gift. But the horse was full of soldiers, who attacked the Trojans as they slept.

These soldiers were called hoplites.

Helmet with nose protector

Strong, bronze metal armour protected the body.

Warriors

Each city had an army, and war was part of daily life. Soldiers had to buy their own weapons and armour, so they often came from rich families.

Greek mythology

The Greeks told many stories about their gods and goddesses.

 Zeus was king of the gods and chief of the 12 gods who lived on Mount Olympus.

 Athena was goddess of war, wisdom, and Athens. She helped heroes in battle.

 Poseidon was the brother of Zeus and Hades and god of the seas and earthquakes.

 Aphrodite was goddess of love and beauty. She loved Ares, the god of war.

 Hades was god of the Underworld – the home of the dead in Greek legends.

Shield

Some shields were decorated with crests.

These leg guards are called greaves.

The Romans

Ancient Rome began as a group of small villages along the River Tiber in Italy. It soon grew into a great and powerful city that ruled a mighty empire.

The Forum

The city of Rome

The city of Rome is still a busy place, just as it was in ancient times. If you visit Rome today, you can see the ruins of the Forum, the Colosseum, and many other splendid Roman buildings.

Gladiators

The Colosseum was a huge building in Rome where people went to watch wild beast shows and gladiator fights. Gladiators often fought to the death.

Gladiators were armed with nets and spears, or small shields and swords.

50,000 people could sit and watch the fights in the arena.

Lions and other wild animals were killed during the shows.

What was a Roman villa?

Latin language

The Romans spoke a language called Latin. Roman children learnt to write Latin by scratching out letters on wooden boards that were covered in wax.

This inscription is written in Latin.

The Roman Empire

The Romans conquered a vast empire. They built this wall between Scotland and England to protect the boundary of their empire.

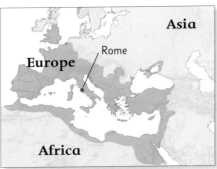

The purple area on this map shows the size of the Roman Empire in about AD 300.

Hadrian's Wall

Famous Romans

Below, you can read about some of the most famous Romans of all.

 Spartacus was a slave who led an army of slaves against the Romans.

 Julius Caesar was a great general who ruled Rome. He was murdered.

 Augustus was the first Roman emperor. After his death, he was made a god.

 Ovid was a Roman poet. He wrote many poems about myths and legends.

 Hadrian toured the empire and built walls and forts to guard it.

The Roman army

The Romans had the best army in the world. Their soldiers conquered many countries and guarded the empire. The soldiers often had to march long distances.

A soldier's sandals

A standard (army flag)

Roman roads

In peacetime, Roman soldiers were kept busy building roads. Roads were important for moving the army around the empire. Roman roads were usually very straight. Some are still used today.

53

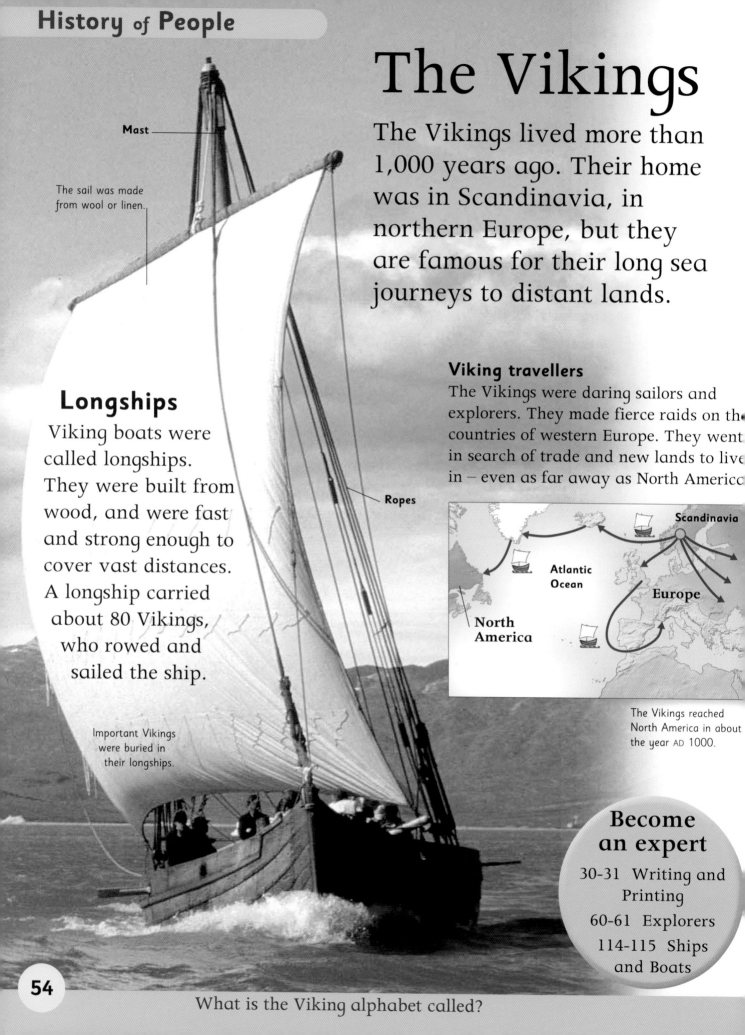

The Vikings

The Vikings lived more than 1,000 years ago. Their home was in Scandinavia, in northern Europe, but they are famous for their long sea journeys to distant lands.

Mast

The sail was made from wool or linen.

Ropes

Longships

Viking boats were called longships. They were built from wood, and were fast and strong enough to cover vast distances. A longship carried about 80 Vikings, who rowed and sailed the ship.

Important Vikings were buried in their longships.

Viking travellers

The Vikings were daring sailors and explorers. They made fierce raids on the countries of western Europe. They went in search of trade and new lands to live in – even as far away as North America.

Scandinavia

Atlantic Ocean

North America

Europe

The Vikings reached North America in about the year AD 1000.

Become an expert

What is the Viking alphabet called?

Warrior duty

Being a brave warrior was very important to the Vikings. They could be called up to fight at any moment, so they always dressed ready for battle.

Viking homes

Viking families lived in houses made from wood, stone, or turf. A hole was left in the roof to let out smoke from the cooking fire. People sat on stools or benches around the fire and slept on raised beds.

Iron and wood spear

Viking warriors carried wooden shields and wore armour made from leather or chain mail.

Helmet with noseguard

Chain-mail shirt

Story-telling

To entertain each other, the Vikings told long stories about their heroes, gods, and great warriors. The stories were called sagas.

A small statue of a Viking god called Frey

Padded leather tunic

Runes

The Vikings carved poems and inscriptions using symbols called runes. Each rune was made of straight lines, so it was easy to carve them on wood or stone.

Round wooden shield

Swords and spears were used for fighting.

Iron sword

Long woollen socks

Goat-skin shoes

Aztecs, Incas, and Mayas

Three great civilizations grew up in the ancient Americas. They were called the Aztecs, Mayas, and Incas These people built great cities and temples to their gods.

Aztec warrior headdress

Where did they live?
The Aztecs and Mayas ruled large parts of Mexico and Central America. The Inca Empire stretched along the west coast of South America.

Aztecs
Mayas
Incas

Aztec temple

Aztec temples looked like pyramids, with steps leading to a shrine on top Here, the Aztecs killed people and offered their hearts to the god of the Sun.

This is Chicomecoatl, the Aztec goddess of maize.

Gods and farming
The Aztecs prayed to the gods to make their crops grow. Most important was maize (corn). It was ground into flour for making flat breads called tortillas.

How were the Incas like the ancient Egyptians?

Spanish galleon

Spanish invasion

In the 16th century, Spanish explorers came to the Americas. Their arrival meant the end of the Aztec, Maya, and Inca empires. Many people were killed and their cities destroyed.

Inca gold

The Incas made objects from gold. The Spanish greed for gold led to the end of the Inca empire.

Llamas were important to the Incas. They were used for wool and for transport.

Gold armbands may have been worn by the bravest Inca warriors.

Statues of Inca gods were made from gold to show honour towards them.

Mayan cities

The Maya built great cities, filled with magnificent stone temples, palaces, and squares. This is the Temple of the Great Jaguar in the Mayan city of Tikal.

Tikal is in Guatemala, South America.

get Mucky

Make an Aztec headdress from card. Cut a circle of card to fit your head and stick on card feathers. Paint it and tape the ends together.

Inca farmers

This is the Inca city of Machu Picchu, high in the Andes mountains in Peru. Farmers grew crops in level fields cut into the mountainside. Maize, legumes (beans), and squash were their main crops.

Ruins of Machu Picchu's buildings can still be seen in Peru today.

They made mummies.

Knights and Castle

Even for brave knights, attacking a castle was dangerous. Thick walls kept them out, and the castle archers had their bows and arrows at the ready.

Types of castle

The first castles were made from wood, but stone was stronger.

French chateaux were magnificent royal homes, with moats and towers.

Norman keeps were stone towers, surrounded by thick castle walls.

Japanese castles were built by warrior lords and had decorative roofs.

The **Red Fort** in India was a palace with stone walls 30 m (100 ft) tall.

Castle design

Massive walls and towers made castles almost impossible for enemy soldiers to attack. Many castles were built on hills, so they were difficult to reach.

Battlements

Tower

Thick walls

get Mucky

Make a knight's shield from a big piece of coloured card. Decorate the shield with your own coat of arms, cut out of silver paper.

Jousting

In peacetime, knights fought practice battles, called jousts, to train for war. They used poles (lances) to knock each other off their horses.

What was chain mail?

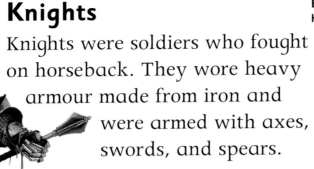

Helmet

Leg guard (greave)

Spur

Knights

Knights were soldiers who fought on horseback. They wore heavy armour made from iron and were armed with axes, swords, and spears.

A knight used his sword to stab between the gaps in an enemy's armour.

Samurai warriors

In Japan, knights were called samurai. They were warriors who fought for a powerful lord and followed a strict code of honour.

Buffalo horns

Samurai warriors wore armour made from coated wood or plates of metal laced together.

Samurai sword

Leather leg protector

Archers fired arrows through slits in the walls.

Lance

Each knight had his own pattern, called his coat of arms.

Shield

Portcullis

Moat

Armour made from small loops of metal.

59

Explorers

For thousands of years, people have set out to explore far-off places. Some explorers hoped to find new lands or goods to trade. Others wanted an adventure.

Early explorers

Thousands of years ago, people called the Polynesians explored the vast Pacific Ocean. They sailed in fragile canoes like this one, and settled on the Pacific islands.

Great expeditions

These are some of the greatest and most daring explorers.

Marco Polo travelled overland from Italy to China in the 13th century.

Burke and **Wills** were the first to cross Australia from south to north in 1860.

Lewis and **Clark** travelled across the USA from east to west in 1804–06.

Magellan led the first mission to sail around the world in the 16th century.

The Santa María

The Santa María was the leading ship of Columbus' expedition.

Columbus' other two ships were called the Niña and the Pinta.

Christopher Columbus

In August 1492, Christopher Columbus set out from Spain, hoping to sail to Asia. In October, he saw land, but it was not Asia. Columbus had reached the new world of the Americas.

Which Italian explorer is America named after?

The South Pole

The first person to reach the icy South Pole was the Norwegian explorer Roald Amundsen, in December 1911. He beat a rival British expedition, led by Captain Robert Scott, by just a month.

Amundsen and one of his team taking photographs at the South Pole in 1911

Mount Everest

In May 1953, Edmund Hillary and Tenzing Norgay became the first people to climb to the top of Mount Everest, the highest mountain on Earth.

This hood was worn by Ernest Shackleton on his attempt to reach the South Pole in 1907–08.

This equipment is from Captain Scott's expedition

Knife

Mug

Shaving mirror

Matches

~The lookout spotted land from his "crow's nest" high up on the mast.

Exploring the deep

Scientists use submersibles (small submarines) to explore the ocean floor and look for sunken ships. They have discovered features and animals never seen before.

NAUTILE

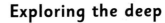
Amerigo Vespucci.

20th century

The 20th century was the time from 1901 to 2000. In the 20th century there were many events, inventions, and discoveries that changed people's lives for ever.

British air force symbol

A British fighter aircraft from World War II

World wars

There were two terrible world wars during the 20th century. World War I lasted from 1914 to 1918. World War II lasted from 1939 to 1945. Millions of soldiers and civilians died in these wars.

Nuclear power

The first nuclear power station was opened in 1954. Today, ther are about 400 of them in the world. These power stations mak dangerous waste. Some people think they should be closed dowr

Nearly three-quarters of France's electricity is made at nuclear power stations. This one is on the River Seine.

This is Sirius, a ship owned and used by the Greenpeace organization

Thick armour protects the tank.

The tracks stop the heavy tank sinking into mud.

Tank

Who was the first person to go into space? And when?

Pop music

The Beatles were one of the most successful pop groups of all time. In the 1960s, millions of people bought their records. Performances on television also helped to boost their fame. The Beatles split up in 1970.

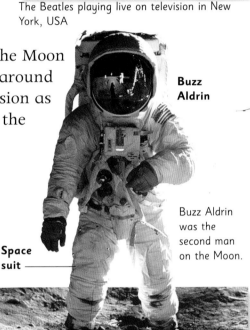

The Beatles playing live on television in New York, USA

Man on the Moon

In 1969, astronauts visited the Moon for the first time. People all around the world watched on television as the astronauts stepped onto the Moon's grey, dusty surface.

Buzz Aldrin

Buzz Aldrin was the second man on the Moon.

Space suit

Advances

Advances made in the 20th century made many people's lives easier.

Mobile telephones and the **Internet** make it easy to keep in touch.

Medical advances help us to fight diseases and recover from injuries.

Inventions such as the jet engine have made travel fast and cheap.

Sport became extremely popular, and many sports people became very famous.

Scientific discoveries, such as DNA, helped medicine and technology.

The environment

Some people began to worry about the damage that humans are doing to the environment. They formed organizations such as Greenpeace and Friends of the Earth.

Nelson Mandela

There were many important political changes during the 20th century. Nelson Mandela fought against an unfair political system in South Africa. He became president of South Africa in 1994.

Technology

Many new types of technology were developed in the 20th century. Microchips were invented in the 1950s. They are used in computers, televisions, stereos, and many other machines.

A Russian cosmonaut (astronaut) called Yuri Gagarin. In 1961.

World of Life

Anything living, such as plants and animals, makes up the living world. It is the world that is all around you – an amazing place to be.

Plants

Plants range from brightly coloured flowers to massive trees. Plants keep us alive. Without plants, we would have nothing to eat and no oxygen to breathe.

Animals can be big and furry...

Many plants grow flowers with bright colours and sweet smells.

Bluebells

Brown bear

Fly agaric toadstools

Fungi

Mushrooms and toadstools are fungi. Fungi are not animals or plants – they are a separate group of living things. Never pick fungi to eat – some are poisonous.

What is a grizzly bear?

Animals

Animals are different from plants because they have to find their own food. Plants can make their own food. Some animals eat plants, and some eat other animals.

Humans

You are a type of animal, too – an animal called a human. There are billions of humans in the world, but there is no one quite like you.

Brown bears belong to a group of animals called mammals. They weigh 500 kg (1,100 lb) and are very strong.

...or small and delicate.

Bears use their sharp claws to dig up roots and to hunt for other animals to eat.

Curiosity quiz

Look through the Living World pages and see if you can identify each of the picture clues below.

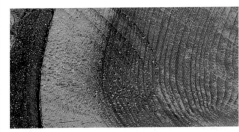

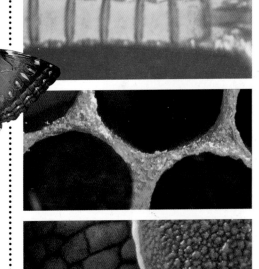

Turn and learn

14-15 Rainforests
98-99 Energy
124-125 Our Planet
134-135 Water

A grizzly bear is another name for a brown bear.

Plant life

The world is home to more than 350,000 different kinds of plants, from tiny sea plants to towering trees.

Flowering plants

Some plants grow colourful flowers. The flower part is important, as it makes the seeds needed to grow new plants.

Fresh air

Plants take in a gas called carbon dioxide, which the use to make their food (see page 70). They give off a gas called oxygen, which humans and animals need to breathe.

Plant life keeps the planet healthy.

Flower

Petal

Bees and other insects eat sugary flower nectar. They help to carry pollen from plant to plant.

Leaf

Which flower stinks of rotting meat?

Making seeds

Plants make seeds so that new plants can grow.

Petals are the bright parts of flowers. They attract insects and animals that carry pollen and seeds.

Pollen is the yellow, dusty stuff that seeds grow from. It is carried from one plant to another.

Seeds travel on animals, water, and the wind to reach the place where they will grow into new plants.

Meat-eating plants

The Venus fly-trap is a plant that eats meat. It traps insects inside its spiky leaves and turns them into liquid food.

Growing

Seeds grow once they reach the earth. A root grows downwards into the soil, and a shoot grows up towards the sunlight.

Plants use their roots to suck up water and food from the soil.

A damselfly

Cactus plants

Cacti grow in hot, dry deserts. They store water in their thick, stubby stems and use it to grow. Because of their prickly spines, very few animals are able to eat cacti.

The leaves snap shut if an insect touches them.

Venus fly-trap

Water-based plants

Some plants live in water. Water lily leaves float on the pond surface, while their roots grow in mud on the bottom.

get Mucky

Make a miniature garden inside a jar or tin. Fill it with soil, then plant some pips, or seeds. Water them well and watch them grow.

Stem  Leaf

The giant rafflesia. It is also the world's biggest flower.

Trees and Forests

A tree is a plant with a thick, woody stem called a trunk. Some trees grow in huge groups, called forests. Forests grow all over the world.

Leaves from broad-leaved trees come in different shapes and sizes.

Beech

Oak

Maple

A wood in Scotland during the autumn

Palm fronds

Broad-leaved trees

Oaks, maples, and beech trees have wide, flat leaves. They lose their leaves in winter. In autumn, the dying leaves turn a lovely golden-brown colour, like the ones shown above.

Become an expert

14-15 Rainforests
134-135 Water
138-139 Climate and Seasons

Record-breaking trees

The tallest trees are giant coast redwoods, like the one shown here from California, USA. They grow to more than 110 m (361 ft) tall.

This giant tree has been hollowed out so that cars can drive through it.

How old is the oldest tree in the world? And what type of tree is it?

onifers

onifers, such as pine and fir trees, are trees hat have needles and cones instead of eaves, flowers, and fruits. They grow in the older parts of the world.

A fir tree branch with needles

Brown fir cones

Conifer forest in winter

The trunk of a tree is made from tough, hard wood.

Palm trees

Palm trees have tall, skinny trunks that bend and sway in the wind. They have huge, fringed leaves called fronds. Palm trees usually grow in warm places.

A coconut

People drink the liquid inside, and eat the white parts.

Useful trees

Many useful things come from trees. Rubber comes from rubber trees. Dates and coconuts grow on palm trees. The paper used to make this book came from conifer trees.

You can count a tree's growth rings to see how old it is.

The trunk is covered in a layer of bark.

Growth rings

It is 4,700 years old. It is a bristlecone pine.

Plants and Food

How many plants have you eaten today? Animals, including people, rely on plants for food. This is because plants can make their own food from water, air, and sunlight.

Air

water

Sunlight

Food for plant

Plants take water from the soil and a gas called carbon dioxide from the air. They use sunlight to turn the water and gas into sugary food. This process is called photosynthesis

The food chain

Plants use food to grow. People and animals need food, too, but they cannot make their own. So they eat plants, things made from plants, or animals that eat plants.

Juicy fruits

When you munch a juicy apple, you are eating the fruit of an apple tree. The apple's tasty flesh grows around its pips (seeds). Can you think of any other types of fruit that are good to eat?

Apple pips (seeds)

Is a tomato a fruit or a vegetable?

Plants we eat

Here are some of the plants, or parts of plants, that humans eat every day.

Plant seeds and **pips** can be good to eat. These are sunflower seeds.

Beans and **peas** are types of plant seed, which we eat as vegetables.

Leaves and **stems**, such as cabbage, lettuce, and celery, are eaten by humans.

Tubers, such as potatoes, and **roots**, such as carrots, grow underground.

Nuts are another type of plant seed. Some grow inside tough, hard shells.

Fruits, such as apples and oranges, have seeds inside. Many are healthy to eat.

Farming

All over the world, people grow plants to eat on farms and in gardens. This is a wheat field. A tractor is ploughing the field, ready for the wheat seeds to be sown.

Tractor with plough

Grains of rice

Planting crops

In some places, crops are still planted and picked by hand. These farmers in Thailand are planting rice in a paddy field. Most types of rice need plenty of water to grow.

Become an expert

42-43 Working people
90-91 Eating and Digestion
98-99 Energy

Harvesting crops

This machine is called a combine harvester. As it moves along, it collects the wheat stalks. Inside, the wheat is beaten around to separate the grain from the stalks.

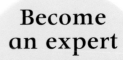
A loaf of wholemeal bread, made from wheat

It is a fruit, because it grows around the seeds.

Animal Groups

There are more than a million types of animal. To make them easier to study, they are divided into groups.

Tiger

Rainbow lorikeet

Birds

Birds are animals with feathers and wings, though not all birds can fly. Baby birds hatch out of hard-shelled eggs, which are often laid in a nest.

Reptiles

Reptiles are animals with dry, scaly skins that mainly live on land. Most baby reptiles hatch out of leathery-shelled eggs, though some reptiles give birth to live young.

Rattlesnake

Snakes, such as this rattlesnake, are types of reptile.

Tree frog

Amphibians

Amphibians are animals that live both in water and on land. They have damp, slimy skins and lay jelly-like eggs. Frogs are amphibians.

Which is the biggest animal ever?

Lion

Mammals

Mammals are animals that mostly give birth to live young and feed their babies on milk. Most mammals have fur or hair on their bodies.

Lions are mammals. Male lions grow bushy manes to make them look bigger and fiercer.

Common fly

Insects

Insects, such as flies, are animals with six legs and a body divided into three parts. Insects are the biggest group of animals, and can live almost anywhere.

A clownfish

Fish

Fish are animals that live in water and breathe through gills. They use their fins to swim. Fish live in the sea, and in lakes, rivers, and ponds.

Curiosity quiz

Look through the Living World pages and see if you can identify each of the picture clues below.

Turn and learn

12-13 Grasslands

86-87 Dinosaurs

134-135 Water

138-139 Climate and Seasons

The blue whale.

Mammals

Mammals are animals with hair or fur on their bodies. They feed their babies on milk. Elephants, bats, whales, wolves, and humans are all mammals.

Once born, mammal babies feed on their mother's milk.

Mammal babies

Most mammals, such as monkeys, cats, and dogs, giv birth to live babies, which look like their parents. The babies grow inside their mother's body until they are born.

Even when older, a joey (young kangaroo) may jump into its mother's pouch for safety.

Mammals with pouche

Some mammals, such as kangaroos and koalas, have pouches on their tummies. Tiny baby kangaroos crawl into their mother's pouch to feed on milk and grow.

Mother and baby gorilla

Which is the fastest mammal on Earth?

Sea mammals

Whales, dolphins, and seals are mammals that live in the sea. They have sleek bodies for swimming and flippers instead of arms and legs. They come to the surface to breathe the air.

Humpback whales

Flying mammals

Bats swoop through the air, looking for insects and fruits to eat. A bat's wings are made from leathery skin stretched across its long fingers.

Here is the bat's furry mammal body.

Primates

Mammals such as monkeys, apes, and human beings are called primates. There are lots of different types of monkey, but the only types of ape are chimpanzees, gorillas, orang-utans, and gibbons.

A young human

Fur coats

Mammals have fur coats for warmth and for camouflage (hiding).

An **arctic fox's** coat turns white in winter to hide it in ice and snow.

Cheetahs have spotty coats that make them hard to see as they stalk prey.

Yaks live high up on cold mountains. A thick, shaggy coat keeps them warm.

A **zebra's** stripy coat hides it in the herd, and makes it hard for hungry lions to see.

A hibernating dormouse

Eastern grey kangaroo and joey

Hibernation

Some mammals sleep all through winter, when it is cold and there is not much to eat. This is hibernation. When spring comes, they wake up to search for food.

A short-beaked echidna (spiny anteater) from Australia

Mammals that lay eggs

Spiny anteaters and duck-billed platypuses are very unusual mammals. Their babies hatch from eggs. Spiny anteaters lay their eggs in a tiny pouch on their tummies. Platypuses lay their eggs in a riverbank nest.

Echidna egg

The cheetah. It can sprint at more than 100 km/h (62 mph).

Amphibians

Frogs, toads, newts, and salamanders are amphibians. Most kinds can live both in water and on land. They all have to be in water to lay their eggs.

This toad's patterned skin helps to hide it from enemies.

Ornamental horned toad

White's tree frog

Tadpole to frog

Baby frogs go through amazing changes before they become adults.

Frogspawn is the slimy, jelly-like stuff laid by frog It is full of tiny black eggs

Tadpoles hatch from the eggs. At first, they are just round body and a long tai

Small legs grow on the tadpoles and they start to look more like tiny frogs.

Baby frogs are ready to live on land. They leave th pond at a few weeks' old.

Frogs and toads

Frogs usually have smooth skin and long legs for leaping. Most toads have bumpy skin and shorter legs for crawling. This is how you can tell them apart.

Caecilians

This strange creature looks like a worm, but it is an amphibian. A caecilian uses its head to dig in the mud and find worms and insects to eat.

Common European frogs

Newts and salamanders

Newts and salamanders are lizard-like amphibians. The have long bodies, long tails, and short legs. Some live on water, others on land. Some have brightly coloured skins, which show that they are poisonous.

European fire salamander

Frogs have large, bulging eyes and good eyesight.

Which frog is the most poisonous?

With a well-timed hop, the frog...

...leaps out of danger.

Leaping legs

Frogs are expert long-jumpers. The champion is the African sharp-nosed frog, which can leap more than 5 m (16 ft) in a single hop. How far can you jump?

Northern leopard frog

Forward-facing eyes allow tree frogs to handle a tricky climb.

Giant tree frog

ating habits

rogs and toads catch flying nsects by flicking out their ong, sticky tongues. They lso eat worms, slugs, nd snails – which they sually hunt at night.

ee frogs have sticky toes help them climb up the ees where they live.

get Mucky

Ask an adult to help you collect some frogspawn from a pond. Keep it in a large jar and watch the tadpoles hatch. Don't forget to put them back in the pond.

The poison-dart frog.

Reptiles

Reptiles can be tiny lizards or enormous snakes many metres long. Reptiles mostly live in hot places because they need sunshine to keep their bodies warm.

Reptile groups

There are about 6,500 types of reptile alive today. They are split into different groups.

Lizards, like this frilled lizard, which lives in Australia.

Tortoises and **turtles**, like this leopard tortoise from Africa.

Crocodiles and **alligators**, like this American alligator.

Snakes, like this common milksnake from the Americas.

Reptile features

Reptiles come in many shapes and sizes, but they all have scaly skins. They run, walk, slither, and swim. Most reptiles lay eggs, which hatch on land.

Snakes shed their skins from time to time and grow bigger ones.

Emerald tree boa

Record-breaking reptiles

The Komodo dragon (above) is the largest, heaviest lizard. The world's biggest reptile is the massive saltwater crocodile. It can grow to 10 m (33 ft) long and is extremely dangerous.

Hatching from eggs

Most reptiles lay eggs with leathery shells, which babies hatch out of. Here you can see a baby leopard tortoise hatching from its egg. It takes about two days for it to push its way out.

Baby leopard tortoise hatching

Which is the longest snake in the world?

Meat-eaters
Crocodiles and alligators are fierce hunters. They hide underwater, then grab their prey with their sharp, pointed teeth. They eat fish, turtles, birds, and mammals.

Crocodiles grow up to 50 sets of teeth.

Nile crocodile

Long lives
Some reptiles live for longer than most other animals. Tortoises can live for more than 100 years. You can tell their age from the patterns of rings on their shells.

Become an expert
10-11 Deserts
86-87 Dinosaurs
102-103 Light and Colour

Colour change
Many reptiles have green or brown skins to help them hide in the trees or on the ground. Chameleons can even change colour, making them very difficult to see.

The chameleon can swivel its eyes to look behind itself.

Chameleons can be brown, green, or yellow – and all the shades in between.

Oustalet's chameleon

The reticulated python. It can grow to 10 m (33 ft) long.

Fish

Fish live in salty oceans, and in rivers, lakes, and ponds. The whale shark is the biggest type of fish, and the tiny dwarf goby fish is the smallest.

Fish features

Most fish have scaly skins, and fins for swimming through the water. They use gills for breathing underwater. Most fish lay lots of jelly-like eggs, which baby fish hatch out of.

Smooth body for moving through water

Back fin

Eye

Gills

Tail fin

Scaly skin

Seahorse fathers

Male seahorses are good fathers. The female squirts her eggs into a pouch on the male's tummy. A few weeks later, the eggs hatch out and the baby seahorses swim away.

Become an expert

8-9 Seas and Oceans

16-17 Rivers and Lakes

134-135 Water

Male seahorse

Baby seahorses

Flat fish

Flat fish, such as sole and plaice, start off as normal fish shapes. Then their bodies flatten out and both eyes move to the same side of their head. Their shape helps to hide them from enemies as they lie on the sea bed.

How small is the dwarf goby fish?

Self defence

Fish are food for sharks and other sea hunters. Many tricks and features help fish to scare away their enemies.

Porcupine fish (or **puffer fish**) blow themselves up like prickly balloons to avoid being eaten.

Stingrays have needle-sharp spikes on their tails, which they whip around to sting enemies.

Stonefish look like harmless stones or rocks sitting on the sea bed, but they are deadly poisonous.

A shark's sharp teeth can be longer than your fingers.

Sharks can grow new teeth every few weeks.

Sharks and rays

Sharks and rays have skeletons made from tough, bendy cartilage, not bone. It is like the stuff you have in the tip of your nose. Sharks are the fiercest ocean hunters, but very few sharks will attack and eat people.

Smaller than your fingernail.

Bony fish

Most fish have bony skeletons, just like humans do. Some bony fish swim about in huge groups, called shoals. Being part of a crowd helps to hide them from enemies.

Shoal of fish

Birds

Birds live all over the world. Parrots and toucans live in the steamy rainforests. Penguins are at home in icy Antarctica. Birds like robins and thrushes are familiar garden visitors.

Flying birds

Some birds fly long distances to find food and places to nest. The Arctic tern is the champion flier. Each year it flies from the Arctic to the Antarctic and back again – a trip of 40,000 km (25,000 miles)!

Owls can fly silently through the night.

Huge eyes

Barn owl in flight

Long, strong wings

Long flight feathers

Bird features

All birds have wings and most birds can fly, though not all of them. Birds are the only animals with feathers. Their babies hatch from hard-shelled eggs, often laid in nests.

Sharp claws for grabbing animal prey

Sharp, hooked beak

Colourful male frigate bird

Feathers

Feathers keep birds warm and help them to fly. Some feathers are plain brown for camouflage. Others are very colourful and help the bird to attract a mate. Males are often very brightly coloured

Which birds make their nests from mud and spit?

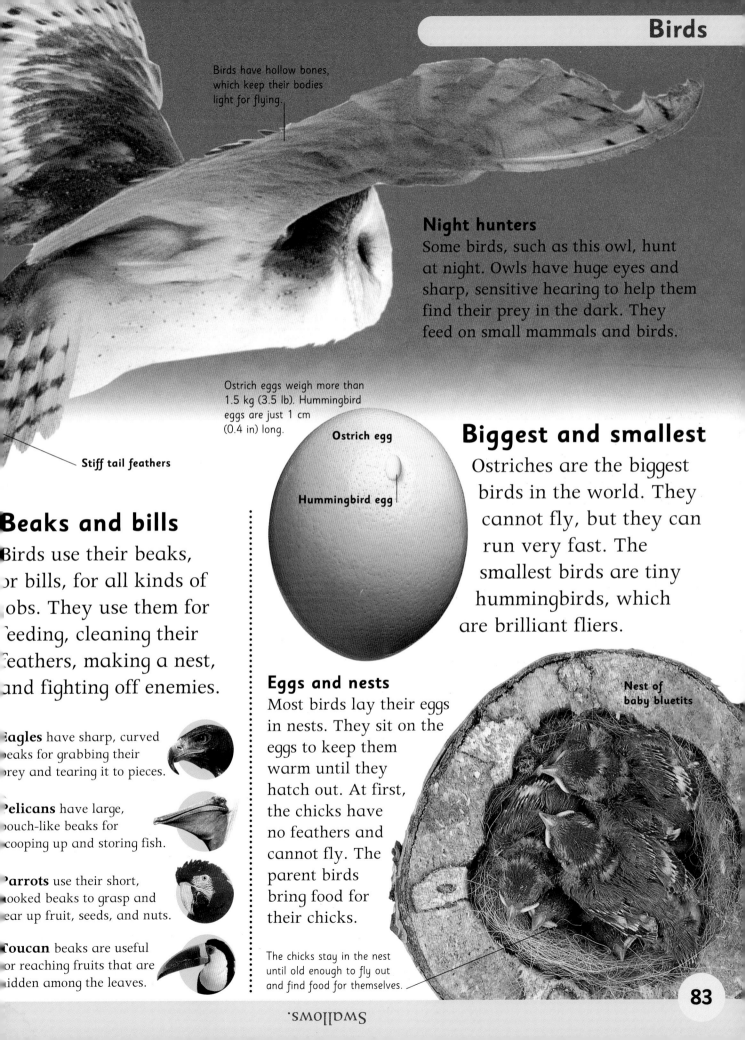

Birds have hollow bones, which keep their bodies light for flying.

Stiff tail feathers

Night hunters

Some birds, such as this owl, hunt at night. Owls have huge eyes and sharp, sensitive hearing to help them find their prey in the dark. They feed on small mammals and birds.

Ostrich eggs weigh more than 1.5 kg (3.5 lb). Hummingbird eggs are just 1 cm (0.4 in) long.

Ostrich egg

Hummingbird egg

Biggest and smallest

Ostriches are the biggest birds in the world. They cannot fly, but they can run very fast. The smallest birds are tiny hummingbirds, which are brilliant fliers.

Beaks and bills

Birds use their beaks, or bills, for all kinds of jobs. They use them for feeding, cleaning their feathers, making a nest, and fighting off enemies.

Eagles have sharp, curved beaks for grabbing their prey and tearing it to pieces.

Pelicans have large, pouch-like beaks for scooping up and storing fish.

Parrots use their short, hooked beaks to grasp and tear up fruit, seeds, and nuts.

Toucan beaks are useful for reaching fruits that are hidden among the leaves.

Eggs and nests

Most birds lay their eggs in nests. They sit on the eggs to keep them warm until they hatch out. At first, the chicks have no feathers and cannot fly. The parent birds bring food for their chicks.

Nest of baby bluetits

The chicks stay in the nest until old enough to fly out and find food for themselves.

Insects and Spiders

Insects and spiders live all over the world. There are more than a million types of insect – more than all other animal types put together.

Jewelled frog beetle

Head

Thorax

Abdomen

One of six legs

Wing

Adult ants are fast movers, but most do not have wings and cannot fly.

Insect features

An insect has six legs. Its body is divided into three parts, called the head, thorax, and abdomen. Its body is sometimes covered in a hard case. Also, many insects have wings.

Insect workers

Hundreds of honey bees live in a home called a hive. Some of the bees are the "workers". They collect sweet nectar from flowers for making honey.

Ants

Types of insect

Most insects are quite small, but they come in a wide range of shapes and colours. Grasshoppers, moths, flies, ants, and bees are all types of insect.

A ladybird's bright colours warn birds that it is not good to eat.

Which insects sing to each other?

utterfly life cycle

Many insects, such as this European swallowtail butterfly, go through amazing changes as they grow.

Egg: the female lays her eggs on a leaf. They hatch into caterpillars.

Caterpillar: the caterpillar feeds on the leaf and grows bigger.

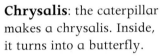

Chrysalis: the caterpillar makes a chrysalis. Inside, it turns into a butterfly.

Adult: the chrysalis splits open and the butterfly struggles out.

European swallowtail butterfly

The eye-shaped markings on this butterfly's wings scare off hungry predators.

Spider features

It is easy to tell insects and spiders apart. A spider has eight legs, instead of six. Its body is divided into two parts, not three.

A spider's head and thorax are joined together.

One of eight legs

Red kneed tarantula

Spinning webs

Many spiders spin webs from silk and use them to catch their supper. Any insect that flies into the web gets caught in the sticky silk. Then, the spider pounces.

Spider relations

They might look very different, but scorpions, ticks, and mites are closely related to spiders. Some scorpions have a deadly sting at the tip of their tail.

Sting

Scorpion

Slug

Millipede

Minibeasts

These creepy-crawlies look like insects, but they are not. Can you see why? Do they have six legs, three parts to their bodies, or wings?

Earthworm

Woodlice

Centipede

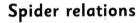

Brachiosaurus

Dinosaurs

Dinosaurs were reptiles that lived on Earth from about 225 to 65 million years ago. We know what they looked like from fossils.

Meat-eaters

Some dinosaurs killed other animals to eat. The terrifying Tyrannosaurus rex had massive jaws lined with dagger-like teeth for ripping apart its prey.

Dinosaur dates

Scientists divide the time when the dinosaurs lived into these three periods.

Triassic: dinosaurs such as this Herrerasaurus lived from 250 to 208 million years ago.

Jurassic: dinosaurs such as this Stegosaurus lived from 208 to 146 million years ago.

Cretaceous: dinosaurs such as this Iguanodon lived from 146 to 65 million years ago.

What does the word "dinosaur" mean?

Troodon

Egg shells

Dinosaur babies

Dinosaurs laid eggs. Some female dinosaurs made nests for their eggs and looked after their young when they hatched. These little dinosaurs are Troodons, which have just hatched out from their eggs.

Dinosaur features

Many plant-eating dinosaurs had special features to protect themselves from hungry meat-eaters. Hunters used deadly disguises to help them sneak up on their prey.

Styracosaurus used its long nose horn to charge at enemies.

Velociraptor probably had blotchy skin to disguise it in its desert home.

Corythosaurus may have used its head crest to scare off rival males.

Death of the dinosaurs

About 65 million years ago, the dinosaurs died out. Some experts think that they starved to death after a giant meteorite hit the Earth.

This huge crater was made by a meteorite that hit the Earth.

Brachiosaurus used its long neck to reach leaves high up in the trees.

Plant-eaters

Many of the largest dinosaurs ate plants. Giants like this plant-eating Brachiosaurus weighed as much as 12 elephants.

Stegosaurus

Smallest brain

Stegosaurus was a plant-eating dinosaur that grew up to 9 m (29 ft) long. But this giant had a tiny brain, only about the size of a walnut.

Terrible lizard.

Human Body

Look in the mirror. What can you see? You
see your body, and it is an amazing thing.
Think of all the things your body can do,
such as running, jumping, and singing.

Everyone has different fingerprints

...because everyone is different.

What colour is your
hair? Hair grows
from your skin.

Are your eye
blue, brown, gree
or grey – or
mixture of two
these colours

Your whole body
is covered in skin.
It is tough and
waterproof.

Wearing
clothes helps
to keep us
warm or cool.

Your skin
and muscle
help you t
pull a face

Where is your thickest skin?

Body map

Your body is made of many different parts. Each part has an important job to do. The parts work together to keep you alive and healthy.

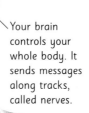
Brain

Your two lungs take oxygen from the air so that you can breathe.

Spine

Your brain controls your whole body. It sends messages along tracks, called nerves.

Lung   Lung

Kidneys

Arm muscles

Skeleton

Your skeleton has more than 200 bones. It helps you to move about and holds your body in shape. Your bones also protect other body parts.

Lots of tiny bones in your hands help you to write and pick up things.

Your blood

Your blood carries food and oxygen to all parts of your body.

Leg muscles

The heart pumps blood all around your body through veins and arteries.

Red blood cells pick up oxygen, which the body needs, from your lungs.

White blood cells help your body to fight disease.

Platelets are tiny bits of cells that plug up a wound.

Leg bones

Foot bones

Curiosity quiz

Look through the Living World pages and see if you can identify each of the picture clues below.

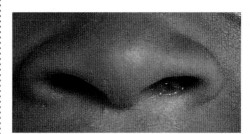

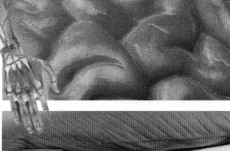

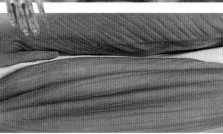

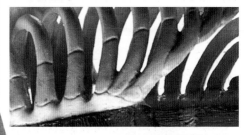

Turn and learn

64-65 World of Life

98-99 Energy

134-135 Water

On the soles of your feet.

Become
an expert
64-65 World of Life
70-71 Plants
and Food
98-99 Energy

Eating and Digestion

Your body needs food to keep it working.
But before it can use the food, it breaks
it into tiny pieces, which seep into your
blood. This is called digestion.

Teeth
Tongue

Mouth

In your mouth,
your teeth chop up
and chew your food. Your spit helps
to break food down and makes it easy
to swallow. When you swallow,
your food goes down a tube
in your throat and into
your stomach.

Your food travels through your body…

This tube diagram is not
the same shape as the
tubes inside your body.

Stomach

Your stomach is like a
stretchy bag that fills with
food. Inside, your food is
churned up and mixed with
stomach juices. They break
your food down into a thick
soup-like mixture.

This photograph of
part of the stomach
lining was taken
through a microscope.

Why does your stomach rumble?

Intestines

Next, your food goes into long tubes called your intestines. It seeps through the walls of the intestines into your blood. Your blood takes the nutrients (goodness) in the food around your body.

Small intestine

This intestine is called your "small" intestine because it is narrow. In fact, it is as long as a bus!

You get rid of waste water and solid waste when you go to the toilet.

Intestine

Stomach

Small intestine

Large intestine

Your small and large intestines are coiled up inside your abdomen.

A meal takes about three days to pass all the way through your digestive system.

Your mouth, stomach, and intestines are called your digestive system.

Getting rid of waste

Any waste food travels from your small intestine into your large intestine. It is stored there until you go to the toilet and push it out as solid waste.

A balanced diet

You need to eat a mixture of foods to keep you strong and healthy. This is called a balanced diet.

Vitamins in fruit and vegetables keep your body working properly.

Fibre in wholemeal bread keeps your digestive system working.

Fat in butter and cheese gives you energy. Too much fat is bad for you.

Carbohydrates such as pasta, rice, and bread give you lots of energy.

Protein in milk helps you to grow and to repair your body.

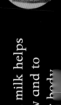

Because of air mixed up with your food.

Muscles and Movement

Your body can run, jump, skip, and hop. This is because the bones and muscles inside you work together to make your body move.

Skull

Your skeleton is made of more than 200 bones.

The skeleton

There are hard, knobbly bones under your skin. They are joined together to make up the bony structure called your skeleton.

Ribs

Pelvis

This skeleton shows how your bones move as you run.

92

Where are your smallest bones and muscles?

Your muscles

All over your skeleton are rubbery muscles. They are fixed to your bones by straps called tendons. Your muscles pull on your bones to make you move.

You have about 640 muscles. They make up about a third of your weight.

Making faces

Each time you pull a face, you use lots of different muscles. There are more than 20 muscles in your face.

Smiling uses muscles to pull up the corners of your mouth.

Frowning uses muscles in your forehead to wrinkle up your forehead.

Pulling this face uses a very special muscle – your tongue.

Your triceps muscle pulls on your arm bones to straighten your arm.

Many muscles pull on your bones, but some pull on your skin.

Your biceps muscle is long and relaxed.

Your biceps muscle gets shorter and pulls to bend your elbow.

Biceps muscle

Your triceps muscle relaxes.

Triceps muscle

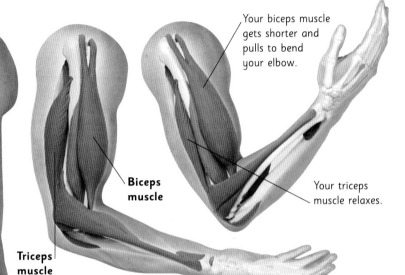

How muscles work

When you want to move your arm, your brain sends a message to your arm muscles. This tells them to get shorter. As they do, they pull on your arm bone and move it.

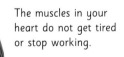

Blood vessel

The muscles in your heart do not get tired or stop working.

Heart

Muscle building

If you do plenty of exercise, you can make your muscles bigger. The biggest muscles in your body are in your bottom and the tops of your legs.

Special muscles

Some muscles do not make you move. Instead, they make you breathe and digest your food. Your heart is a special muscle that pumps blood around your body.

You use your brain to think.

Brain and Senses

Your brain is the part of your body that makes you think, feel, and remember. It makes sure that the rest of you works properly.

Your brain

Your brain is hidden inside your head. It looks a little bit like a soft, wrinkly lump of greyish-pink blancmange, or jelly.

Different parts

A bundle of nerves runs down your back, inside your backbone.

Your hard, bony skull protects your brain from damage.

Nerves

Your brain is linked to your body by fibres called nerves. Nerves carry messages from your body to your brain, and back again.

Your brain weighs about the same as 12 apples.

If you prick your finger, your brain makes you feel pain.

Reflex actions

If you accidentally prick your finger on a rose thorn, your brain quickly makes you pull your hand away. This fast reaction is called a reflex action.

Do clever people have bigger brains?

Your senses

You know what is happening around you by seeing, hearing, smelling, tasting, and touching things. These are called your senses.

...do different jobs.

Your eyes see the pictures, then your brain tells you what they are.

Eyes and seeing

Your eyes have special nerves that pick up light. They send messages to your brain, telling you what you are looking at.

Your ears pick up loud and soft sounds.

Ears and hearing

Your ears catch sounds and send them deep inside your head. Nerves send messages about the sounds to your brain.

Nose and smelling

Nerves inside your nose tell you what you are smelling. Some things, such as this rose, smell nice. Other things smell terrible!

Tongue and tasting

You taste with your tongue. It is covered with tiny bumps, called taste buds, which pick up tastes from your food.

Skin and touch

Nerves in your skin tell you if things feel hard, soft, hot, or cold. They also warn you of danger by making you feel pain.

Brown sugar   **Grapes**   **Spaghetti**

Can you tell what you are touching, without looking?

No. Everyone's brain is about the same size.

World of Science

Do you study science at school? Science helps us to understand the world around us. It also helps us to make medicines, grow more food, make new materials, and protect the environment

Red blood cell

White blood cell

Blood cells seen through a microscope

How scientists work

Scientists must work carefully and in a logical way. They write down how they think something works. This is called a theory. They do experiments (tests) to see if their theories (ideas) are correct.

A microscope lets a scientist examine very tiny things.

Microscope

Science experiments

During experiments scientists take measurements and carefully watch what happens. They write down their findings and decide whether the results prove their theory, or show anything interesting.

What is the name for a scientist who studies dinosaurs?

Theory of materials

An important scientific theory is that all materials are either solids, liquids, or gases.

Solids do not change shape. A piece of rock is a solid.

Liquids flow downwards and take the shape of the container they are in.

Gases are very light. They expand to fill any container they are in.

Scientific theories

Scientists have tested thousands of theories about the world around us. In the 1660s, Isaac Newton wrote down a theory about why things fall downwards – called the theory of gravity.

Gravity pulls everything down towards the Earth.

An apple falls downwards because of gravity.

Gravity makes the apple fall faster and faster.

Gravity

Famous scientists

Some scientists are world famous because they have made amazing discoveries. Albert Einstein (1879-1955) was the most famous scientist of all. He wrote down theories that have helped us to understand the Universe.

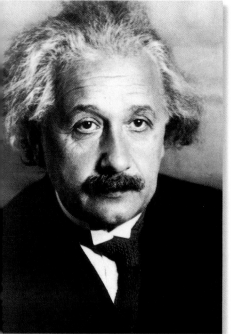

Albert Einstein was brilliant at physics and mathematics.

Curiosity quiz

Look through the Science and Technology pages to identify each of the picture clues below.

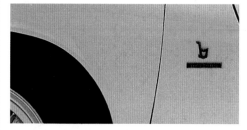

Turn and learn

106-107 Forces and Movement

140-141 The Universe

154-155 Space exploration

A palaeontologist.

Energy

If you did not eat your meals, you would not have enough energy to play games, stay awake, or even think! Energy makes things happen, and nothing can take place without it.

A heavy rollercoaster car has lots of movement energy.

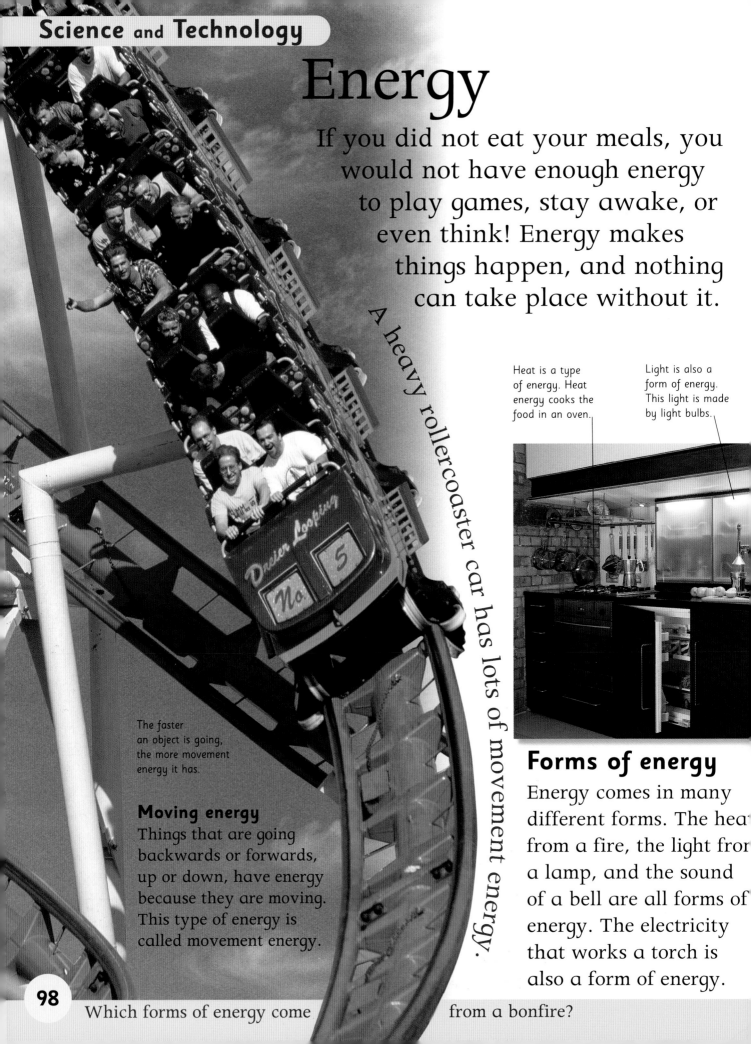

Heat is a type of energy. Heat energy cooks the food in an oven.

Light is also a form of energy. This light is made by light bulbs.

The faster an object is going, the more movement energy it has.

Moving energy

Things that are going backwards or forwards, up or down, have energy because they are moving. This type of energy is called movement energy.

Forms of energy

Energy comes in many different forms. The heat from a fire, the light from a lamp, and the sound of a bell are all forms of energy. The electricity that works a torch is also a form of energy.

Which forms of energy come from a bonfire?

Fuels

Wood, petrol, and coal have energy in them that we can get out. They are called fuels. The energy in petrol makes cars move along.

Filling a car with fuel is like filling it with energy.

You can run a long way using the energy in your breakfast foods.

Energy is stored in your body as fat.

Your muscles turn stored energy into movement.

Milk

Orange juice

Cereal

Apple

Nuts and raisins

Chocolate

Changing energy

Energy can change from one form to another. Here are some changes of energy that we use.

Electric motors change electrical energy into movement energy.

Light bulbs change electrical energy into light energy.

Solar panels change light energy from the Sun into electrical energy.

Drums change movement energy (when you hit them) into sound energy.

Loudspeakers change electrical energy into sound energy.

Food as fuel

All these foods have energy stored in them, ready to be used. For example, an apple tree uses energy from sunlight to grow. Some of this energy is stored in its apples.

Stored energy

Food is fuel for your body. When we eat food, the energy gets stored in our bodies. The energy is released when we need it.

Saving energy

Keeping a house warm in winter uses lots of energy and is expensive. Putting fluffy insulation in the loft helps to stop heat energy from leaking away through the roof.

Heat energy and light energy.

Electricity

What happens when you switch on
a light or turn on your computer?
Electricity starts flowing and makes
the light or the computer work.

Generating stations

Electricity is made at a
generating station. Coal,
gas, or oil are burned to
make heat. Then the heat
is turned into electricity.

Power to your home

Electricity travels to your
home along thick wires.
Some wires hang on
pylons and some are
hidden underground.

Electricity flows to
your home along
wires like these.

Electricity flows along
this copper wire.

The plastic stops
electricity escaping
from the wire.

Conductors
and insulators

Electrical cables are
made of metal and
plastic. The metal lets
electricity flow. It is
called a conductor.
The plastic makes the
cable safe to touch. It
is called an insulator.

The wires
hang from tall
metal towers
called pylons.

Electricity is very
dangerous. Never poke
anything into a socket.

What kind of electricity can you sometimes see in the sky?

Wires carry electricity from a battery to the electromagnet.

Iron bar

Electric magnets

A coil of wire with electricity flowing around it is called an electromagnet. It pulls on metal things, just like an ordinary magnet does. Motors have electromagnets inside them.

Iron filings

Wire is wrapped around the iron bar many times.

Making electricity

Electricity can be made from coal, gas, and oil, or from the sunlight, wind, and water around us.

 Hydroelectric dams use the power of flowing water to make electricity.

 Solar cells are used to turn the energy from sunlight into electricity.

 Wind turbines use the wind to power machines that make electricity.

 Wave generators turn the energy in powerful ocean waves into electricity.

Switch

Wire

Closing the switch completes the circuit so that the electricity can flow.

Electric circuits

An electric circuit is a loop that electricity can flow around. Electricity flows around this circuit to make the two bulbs light up.

The electricity flowing around this circuit comes from two batteries.

Crocodile clip

Light bulb

A light bulb turns electricity into light.

get into it
Rub a party balloon up and down on your clothes. The balloon will now stick to a wall. This happens because of a kind of electricity called static.

A battery is a store of electricity. It pushes electricity around the circuit.

Lightning (static electricity).

Light and Colour

Light is amazing. We can only see things because of the light that enters our eyes. Light comes in lots of beautiful colours.

Light rays
Light travels in straight lines, called rays. Light rays cannot go around corners. If something gets in the way, it blocks the light rays and makes a shadow.

The shadow is the same shape as the object that is blocking the light rays.

Shadow puppet

A shadow is a place where light does not get to.

This puppet is blocking the rays of light from the torch.

You can see yourself in a mirror because light bounces off the glass.

A torch casts dramatic shadows.

Torch

Bouncing light
We see things because light rays bounce off them and into our eyes. Then our eyes send signals to our brain and we see pictures.

Sources of light
Most of the light we see comes from the Sun. Light bulbs, like the one in the torch, use electricity to make light.

What is the fastest thing in the Universe?

Mixing colours

Mixing two different colours together makes a new colour. You can make many different colours for a picture by mixing up just a few colours of paint.

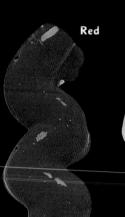
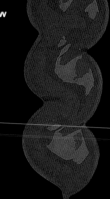

Red

Blue

Yellow

Red, yellow, and blue are called the primary colours of paint.

Colours in light

Light from the Sun is made up of many different colours. When it rains you can see a rainbow, which contains lots of these different colours.

Bending light

When light rays hit a glass surface, the glass makes them bend. A magnifying glass bends light to make things look bigger than they really are.

get Mucky

Try making a rainbow. Stand outside with your back to the Sun and spray water from a garden hose into the air. How many colours can you see?

Blue morpho butterfly

Magnifying glass

The magnifying glass makes the butterfly's wing look much bigger.

Using colours

People, plants, and animals use colours in lots of different ways.

Red means danger. A red line around a sign means "look out"!

Green means "okay". A green light means it is safe to cross the road.

Yellow on this frog's skin means "don't eat me, I'm poisonous!"

Bright feathers help birds, such as this rainbow lorikeet, to attract a mate.

Colourful flowers attract insects and birds, which pollinate them.

103

Light. It travels 300,000 km (186,000 miles) every second.

Sound

Every day, we hear natural sounds, like the wind, and other noises such as cars and aeroplanes. We also put together different sounds to make music.

Sound waves

Making sound

Sounds are made when things vibrate (move quickly back and forth). They make the air vibrate, too. The vibrations spread through the air in waves. We hear the sound when the waves enter our ears.

Sound levels

Loudness is measured in decibels. Very loud sounds can damage ear

Falling leaves make a "rustling" sound of about 20 decibels.

Talking measures abo 60 decibels. Whispering measures about 30.

Vacuum cleaners make noises of between 60 and 80 decibels.

Jet engines are very loud. An aircraft taking off measures 140 decibels.

Percussion instruments

Hitting a metal tray makes the tray vibrate.

Percussion instruments have parts that crash together.

A stringed instrument has vibrating strings.

Loud and quiet sounds

Big vibrations in the air have lots of energy. They sound very loud. Small vibrations in the air have much less energy. They sound very quiet.

The sound waves from the tray make the paper vibrate, which makes the sugar grains on it jump around.

What makes the strings of a violin vibrate?

A bat has large ears to listen for echoes.

Bouncing sounds

Have you ever heard an echo? An echo is made when a sound bounces off a wall or a cliff face. You hear the sound twice. Bats send out high-pitched sounds and listen for their echoes to find prey.

Horseshoe bat

Wind instruments

A drum is a percussion instrument.

The speed of sound

Sound travels very fast. It goes at 1,200 km/h (745 mph) through the air. Things that travel faster than sound are called supersonic. They cause the air to make a loud, booming noise called a sonic boom.

Concorde is a supersonic airliner.

Concorde flies twice as fast as sound.

High and low sounds

Fast vibrations make noises that sound very high, such as a whistle. Slow vibrations make noises that sound low, such as a roar.

Become an expert

34-35 Music
74-75 Mammals
82-83 Birds
94-95 Brain and Senses

A wind instrument makes sound using air that vibrates inside a tube.

Animal sounds

Animals such as birds, dolphins, and dogs use sounds to communicate with each other. Some animals hear sounds that we cannot hear. Dogs can hear very high sounds.

A bow.

Forces and Movement

A force is a push or a pull. When you pull (or push) on a door or on your school bag, or push on your bike's pedals (or its brakes) you are making forces.

Making things move

Forces can change the way things are moving. A force can make a thing start or stop, make it go faster or slower, or make it spin around.

Weighing machines work by measuring the pull of gravity on an object.

Gravity pulls the Moon towards the Earth. It stops the Moon drifting off into space.

Gravity and weight

When you jump in the air, you always fall back to the ground. The force that pulls you down is called gravity. Gravity pulls everything towards the Earth. The weight of something is the force that gravity pulls it down with.

This girl is swinging backwards and forwards because forces are pushing and pulling on her.

Apple

Why do things weigh less on the Moon than they do on the Earth?

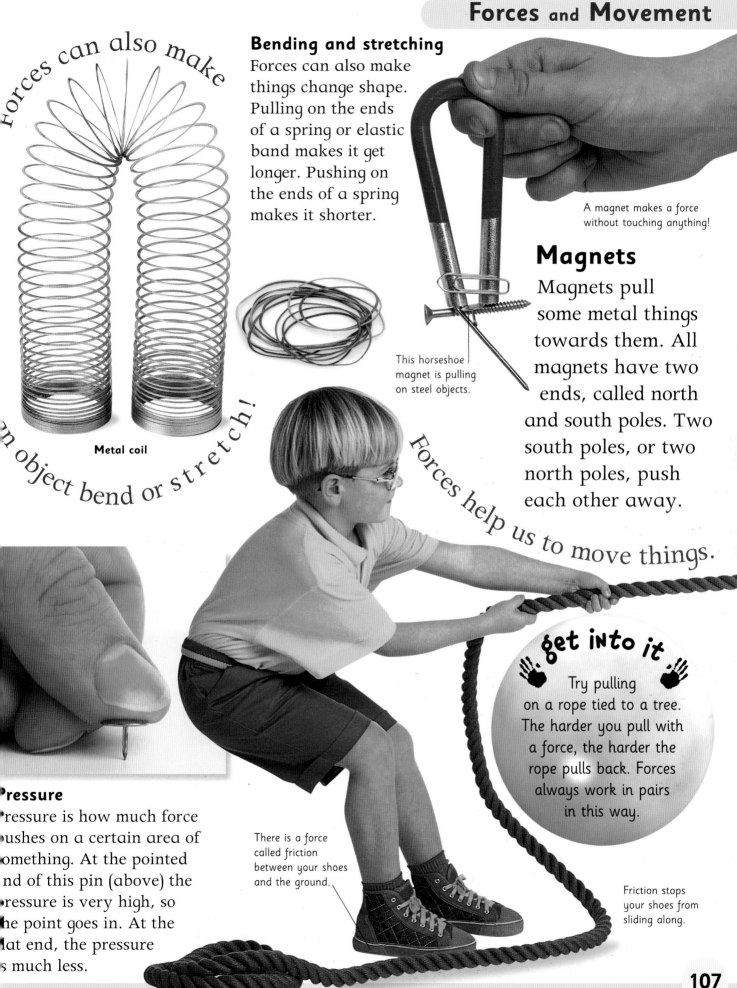

Forces can also make

Bending and stretching
Forces can also make things change shape. Pulling on the ends of a spring or elastic band makes it get longer. Pushing on the ends of a spring makes it shorter.

A magnet makes a force without touching anything!

Magnets
Magnets pull some metal things towards them. All magnets have two ends, called north and south poles. Two south poles, or two north poles, push each other away.

This horseshoe magnet is pulling on steel objects.

Metal coil

n object bend or stretch!

Forces help us to move things.

get into it

Try pulling on a rope tied to a tree. The harder you pull with a force, the harder the rope pulls back. Forces always work in pairs in this way.

Pressure
Pressure is how much force pushes on a certain area of something. At the pointed end of this pin (above) the pressure is very high, so the point goes in. At the flat end, the pressure is much less.

There is a force called friction between your shoes and the ground.

Friction stops your shoes from sliding along.

on the Moon. Because the pull of gravity is weaker

Industry and Invention

The food you eat, the bus you take to school, and the fuel that heats your home are all made by industries. The machines and gadgets you use were all invented by somebody.

A construction worker on a building site

Steel is used in the construction of buildings.

Big industries

Here are some of the world's biggest industrie They produce most of th things we need.

Manufacturing industr make all the machines ar gadgets that we use.

The **mining** industry dig up coal and the rocks tha we get metals from.

Oil and **gas** industries make oil and gas into fuels and other products.

The **construction** indust builds houses, skyscraper bridges, tunnels, and dan

Food and **farming** industries produce crops, meat, and ready-made me

Iron and steel industry

Iron and steel are very important materials that many industries need. Every year, millions of tonnes of iron and steel are made from rocks in the ground.

Who invented Morse code?

Communications inventions

The telephone, satellites, and the internet are all inventions in communications. They make it easy for us to talk to each other.

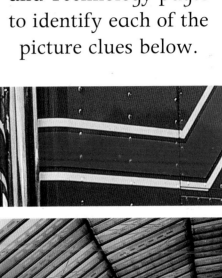

The user spoke into the mouthpiece.

This is the earpiece where the user would listen.

Telephone from the 1920s

small, modern family car

The engine under the bonnet is very powerful. New technology makes these engines less likely to go wrong.

Transport inventions

Jet engines, diesel engines, and hovercraft are all inventions in transport. They help us to travel quickly and safely from place to place.

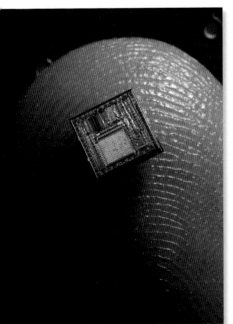

The microchip

If the microchip had not been invented, we would not have personal computers, games consoles, stereos, and many other electronic machines.

Microchips are tiny electronic circuits.

Curiosity quiz

Look through the Science and Technology pages to identify each of the picture clues below.

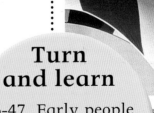

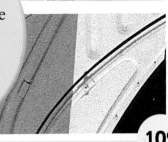

Turn and learn

46-47 Early people

130-131 Earth's materials

152-153 Space travel

109

Samuel Morse.

Cars, Trucks, and Trains

Cars, trucks, and trains are types of vehicle that carry people and goods all around the world. These moving machines travel around on roads and railway tracks.

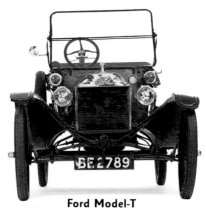

Ford Model-T

The first cars

The first cars were open topped and travelled at slow speeds. A man walked in front with a flag to warn people that a car was coming.

In this car, the engine is kept at the rear.

A car's engine is normally stored under the bonnet.

Metal body

Lamborghini Miura

Rubber tyres grip the road.

Cars today

Modern cars have powerful engines to turn their wheels and strong bodies made from metal. Every year, millions of new cars are built.

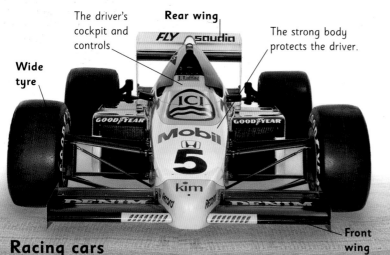

The driver's cockpit and controls

Rear wing

The strong body protects the driver.

Wide tyre

Front wing

Racing cars

This racing car whizzes along at more than 300 km/h (186 mph). Its large, rubber tyres stop it from skidding as it speeds around corners.

Which is the fastest passenger train in the world?

Kinds of car

Cars come in all sorts of shapes and sizes. Here are some fun examples.

Classic cars are old makes of car. Some people collect them to display at shows.

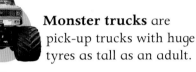

Monster trucks are pick-up trucks with huge tyres as tall as an adult.

Limousines are luxury cars with big, comfy seats inside.

Electric cars have an electric motor instead of an engine.

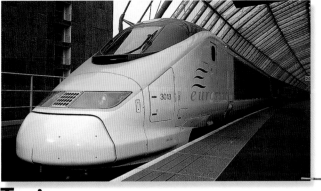

High-speed Eurostar trains travel from Britain to Europe through the Channel Tunnel.

Trains

Trains move along on railway tracks. The first trains had steam engines. Modern trains have electric motors or diesel engines.

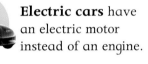

This train was built nearly 200 years ago to pull wagons in mines.

Driver's sleeping compartment

WALKER BROS

This trailer is called a curtain-sided trailer.

Big trucks

The biggest trucks are called articulated trucks. They have a tractor at the front and a trailer at the back, full of cargo.

Lots of big tyres spread out the truck's weight.

Become an expert

98-99 Energy

108-109 Industry and Invention

116-117 Engineering

The Spanish AVE train. It has a top speed of 300 km/h (186 mph).

Ships and Boats

The crew control the ship from a room called the bridge.

Have you been across the sea on a ferry or an ocean liner? Ferries and liners are called ships. Most ships carry cargo. Boats are like ships, but they are smaller.

Containers

Ships

This is a container ship. It carries hundreds of metal containers filled with cargo. The main part of the ship is called the hull. Inside the hull are floors called decks.

Tug boats

A tug is a small, powerful boat that can tow a big ship. The tug boat guides the big ship in and out of the harbour.

The sharp bow pushes through the water.

Become an expert

What is a boat with two separate hulls called?

Boats

There are many types of boat. Some carry goods or passengers, some have special jobs to do, and some are just for fun.

Fishing boats pull huge nets through the water to scoop up fish.

Lifeboats go out in stormy seas to rescue people in trouble.

Hovercraft skim across the top of the sea on a cushion of air.

Jet skis are fun boats that skim and jump across the waves.

Sailboards are like surfboards, but with a mast and sail on top.

Sailing boats

Spinnaker

When the wind blows, you can go sailing. The wind pushes on the boat's sails and makes the boat go forwards. This boat is a big racing yacht. The tall, triangle-shaped sail at the front is called a spinnaker.

Conning tower

Most of the submarine is under the water.

S 190

Submarines

A submarine is a ship that can dive under the water. This fighting submarine (above) carries missiles for attacking enemy ships.

Submersibles

Scientists use small submarines called submersibles to explore the deep sea. This submersible is called Deep Star. It can dive more than 1,200 m (4,000 ft) below the surface of the sea.

Fighting ships

This fighting ship is called a frigate. It has guns and missiles to defend itself against other warships and aircraft. At the back are a helicopter deck and a hangar (a building for storing aircraft).

Fumes from the engine come out of the funnel.

The radar on the mast detects other ships and aircraft.

The gun turret spins around to fire in any direction.

F174

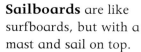

▲ A catamaran.

Engineering

Designing and building things such as cars and towering skyscrapers is called engineering. People who do engineering are called engineers. They have to be good at science and mathematics.

The construction of the Empire State Building in New York, USA

Engineering materials

Engineers use hard-wearing materials, such as metal, plastic, and wood. This picture from the 1930s shows a construction worker building the steel frame of a skyscraper.

Mechanical engineering

Designing and making machines, and parts of machines, is called mechanical engineering. Mechanical engineers also repair machines that have gone wrong.

The construction of an aircraft in a factory

Engineers who make aircraft are called aeronautical engineers.

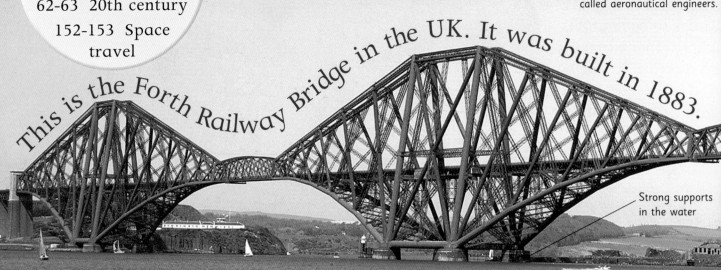

This is the Forth Railway Bridge in the UK. It was built in 1883.

Strong supports in the water

What sort of bridge did ancient Roman engineers invent?

Engineering machines

Parts of machines are often made and fitted together by other machines. This is a car production line. As the cars move past, robots weld them together, then paint them.

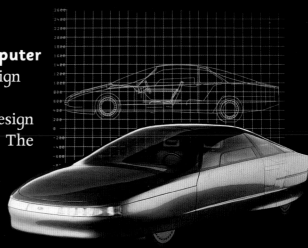

Robots join the car parts together with welding torches.

Engineering in space

Astronauts work in space to mend satellites and build space stations. Space engineering is difficult work because parts float around and the astronauts have to wear bulky space suits and thick gloves.

Designing by computer

Computer-aided design (CAD for short) uses computers to help design things, such as cars. The computer can show what the car will look like before the real car is made.

Civil engineering

Civil engineering is designing and building roads, railways, bridges, tunnels, dams, and tower blocks. Civil engineers work with strong materials, such as steel and concrete.

The bridge is made of huge metal tubes.

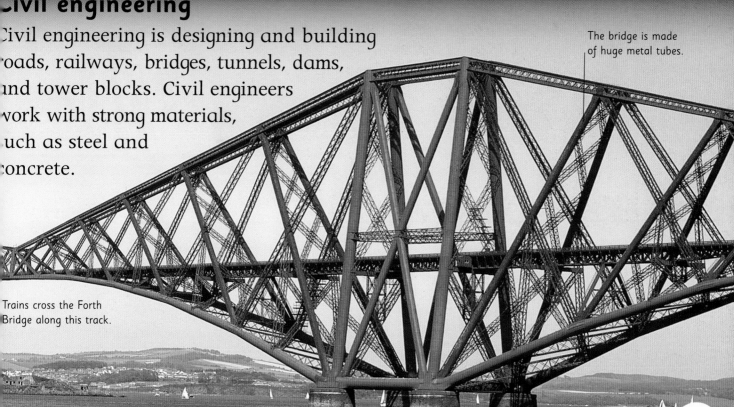

Trains cross the Forth Bridge along this track.

The arch bridge.

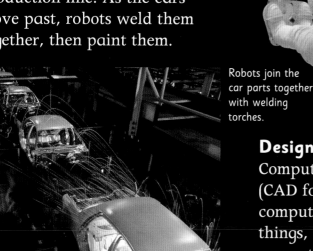

Machines and Computers

Machines are things that help us to do jobs. Machines such as scissors are very simple. Machines such as computers are very complicated.

The crane's "boom" stretch[...] all the way across t[...] building sit[...]

Operator's cab

The shadoof helps this Egyptian farmer to lift a heavy bucket of water.

Simple machines

This simple machine is called a shadoof. It is a type of lever. Farmers use it to put water onto their fields. Tools such as tin openers and pliers are also simple machines

get into it

Rest a ruler on a pencil. Push down on one end of the ruler to lift the other end up. This is a machine called a lever. Levers help to lift weights.

This digger is digging a ditch for a large pipe to go in.

A crane is a machine that lifts and moves heavy loads.

Chunky tyres

What sort of machine pulls a plough on a farm?

The first computers

The first computers were built in the 1940s. They were huge. Some, like this one, filled a whole room. But they could not do as many things as a modern pocket calculator!

This machine was called the Electronic Numerical Indicator and Calculator (ENIAC).

Computer parts

These computer parts let you control a computer and get data in and out.

Monitor: this is a screen where a computer shows words and pictures.

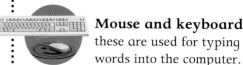
Mouse and keyboard: these are used for typing words into the computer.

Scanner: this turns pictures and photographs into data in the computer.

Printer: this copies words and pictures from the screen onto paper.

Computers

A computer is a machine that stores information, called data, in its memory. A computer has an electronic brain that moves data around very quickly.

Lap-top computer

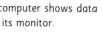

A computer shows data on its monitor.

iBook

This vacuum cleaner spins air around and around to suck dust out of carpets.

Construction machines

You can see lots of big machines on a construction site. They dig holes in the ground and move heavy materials around the site.

Digging arm

Robotic vacuum cleaner

Machines at home

Vacuum cleaners, washing machines, lawn mowers, and hedge cutters are machines that help us to do jobs at home and in the garden. They all have motors inside that move their parts.

Television and Media

Television, radio, newspapers, magazines, and the Internet make up the media. They bring us news, information, and entertainment.

These screens show the pictures from all the cameras.

Television monitor

Television

Presenters, camera operators, sound engineers, directors, an producers are needed to make a television programme. Most programmes are made in room called studios.

A presenter and camera operato making a programme in television studi

The director decide what pictures and sounds we see on our televisions.

When was the first television programme shown?

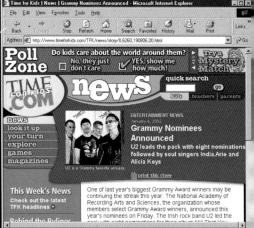

Radio

At the back of this picture is a radio studio. The presenters are speaking into microphones. The person at the front controls what the listeners hear on their radios.

Newspapers

Thousands of local, national, and international newspapers are published every day. There are also weekly and monthly magazines on hundreds of different subjects.

Writing the news

People who find news stories are called journalists. They record what people do or say and write articles that we read in newspapers, or reports for television news programmes.

Daily newspapers from around the world

Many newspapers and TV stations have a multimedia news website on the Internet.

Advertising

You probably see hundreds of adverts every day. Adverts tell us about products or services that companies offer. The companies pay television, newspaper, and magazine companies to show their adverts.

In towns and cities there are adverts almost everywhere you look!

Multimedia

The word "multimedia" means different media mixed together. There are many multimedia websites on the Internet. These sites show words and photographs, and also sounds and moving pictures.

In 1928.

Communications

Communication satellites send messages from one part of the world to another.

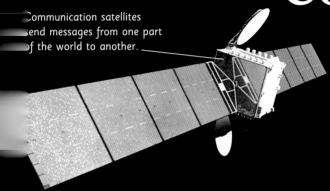

The telephone, television, radio and the Internet are different ways of communicating with people. They let us talk to each other, or send words, pictures, and sounds.

Telecommunications

Television, radio, telephones, and e-mail are called telecommunications. They send messages over long distances. The messages go through underground cables, radio aerials, and satellites.

This huge dish is an aerial. It beams messages to communication satellites and collects the messages that come back.

Simple communications

Here are some ways you could communicate without speaking.

Semaphore uses two flags held in different positions to show letters.

Morse code uses short and long beeps or flashes to show letters.

Puffs of smoke from a fire can show rescuers where someone is.

Sign language uses hand signs to help deaf people communicate.

Blowing a whistle can call for help in an emergency.

Radio

The sounds you hear on a radio travel through the air to the radio as invisible radio waves. The radio picks up the radio waves with its aerial.

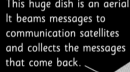

You choose a radio station with the tuning dial.

Which three letters mean "Help!"?

Information by light

Words, pictures, and sounds are often turned into flashes of light for their journey from one place to another. The light travels along special cables called optical-fibre cables.

Telephones

A telephone turns the sound of your voice into signals that can travel as electricity, radio waves, or light. Complicated electronics connect your phone to the one you are calling.

Some mobile phones can send e-mails and look at websites on the Internet.

Light travels along thin threads of glass inside the cables.

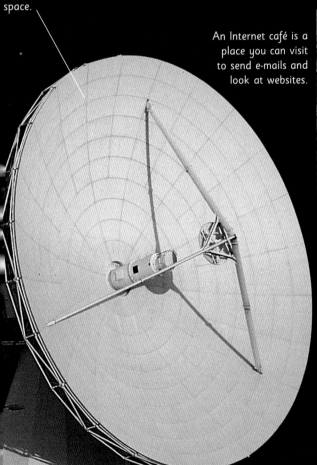

e dish is aimed the satellites space.

The Internet

The Internet is made up of millions of computers all over the world connected together. It lets us send e-mails and look at websites that are stored on the computers.

An Internet café is a place you can visit to send e-mails and look at websites.

Television and video

The word "video" means moving pictures. You can watch video on television or on a computer screen. The pictures are filmed using a video camera.

You might have a television satellite dish at home.

Some video is "live", which means you see it as it is being filmed.

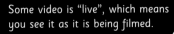

Our Planet

The Earth is the planet where we all live. It is a huge ball of hot, liquid rock with a solid surface called the crust. Planet Earth travels in space.

The Earth's axis goes through its poles.

North Pole

The Earth's axis...

...is tilted to one side.

Sout Pole

Spinning Earth

The Earth slowly spins around once a day. The line it spins around is called the Earth's axis. At the ends of the axis are the Earth's poles.

The Earth's surface

There are seven huge pieces of land on the Earth's surface. They are called continents. They cover about one-third of the surface. Oceans cover the rest.

Earth as a magnet

Have you ever used a compass to find your way? It works because the Earth acts as if it has a giant bar magnet in the middle.

Which is the biggest ocean on the Earth?

Inside the Earth

The Earth's crust is quite thin. Underneath is a layer of hot, molten (melted) rock called the mantle. In the middle is a solid core.

Curiosity quiz

Look through the Planet Earth pages and see if you can identify each of the picture clues below.

The cracked crust

The Earth's crust is cracked into lots of huge pieces called plates. The cracks are called fault lines. Earthquakes and volcanoes often happen where the edges of the plates grind together.

The San Andreas fault, California, USA

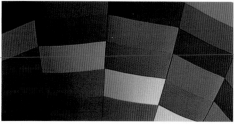

Mountains and valleys

Most mountains are made when rocks are pushed upwards by movements of the Earth's crust. Blowing winds, flowing rivers, and glaciers wear away the mountains.

Sedona, Arizona, south-western USA

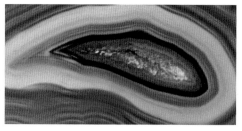

Turn and learn

The Pacific Ocean. It covers nearly half of the Earth's surface.

Volcanoes and Earthquake

The ground under your feet seems very solid, but in places it is weak or cracked. These places are where volcanoes and earthquakes happen.

Flowing lava
The hot, runny rock that flows out of a volcano is called lava. Lava can sometimes travel very fast, like a red-hot river.

Volcanoes are often cone-shaped mountains. The cone is made of hardened lava from the volcano.

Volcanoe
Magma is melted roc under the Earth's crust Sometimes it bursts through a opening in the crust, calle a volcano. Lots of as and dust shoo out, too

What is the name for a large ocean wave caused by an earthquake?

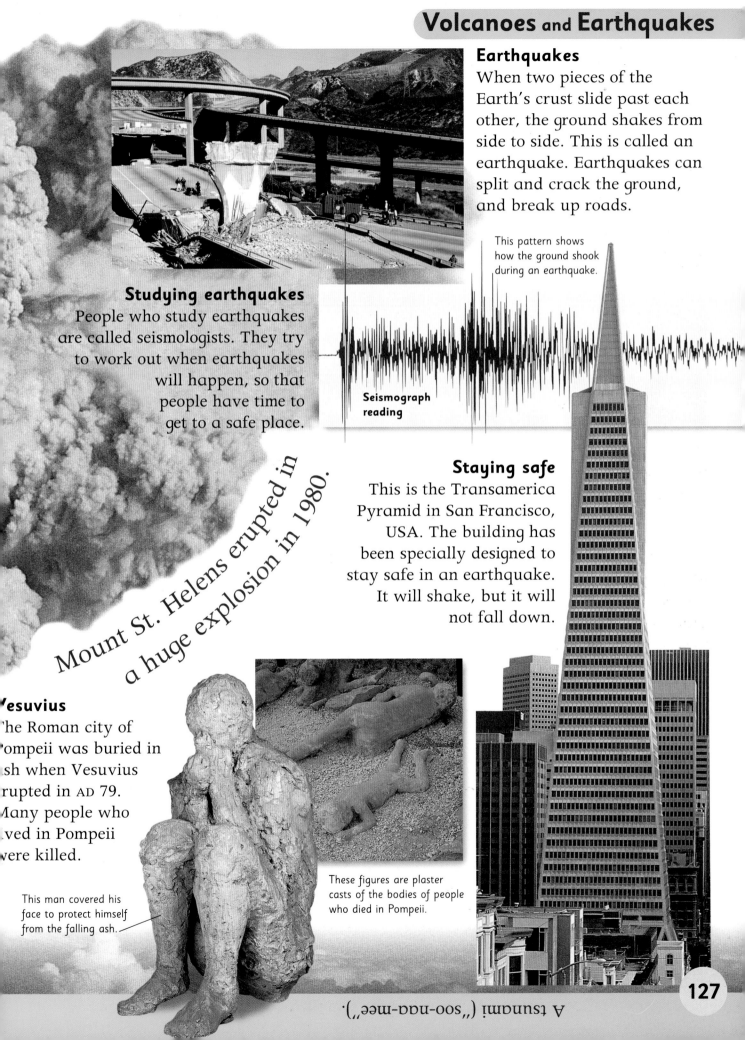

Earthquakes

When two pieces of the Earth's crust slide past each other, the ground shakes from side to side. This is called an earthquake. Earthquakes can split and crack the ground, and break up roads.

Studying earthquakes

People who study earthquakes are called seismologists. They try to work out when earthquakes will happen, so that people have time to get to a safe place.

This pattern shows how the ground shook during an earthquake.

Seismograph reading

Staying safe

This is the Transamerica Pyramid in San Francisco, USA. The building has been specially designed to stay safe in an earthquake. It will shake, but it will not fall down.

Mount St. Helens erupted in a huge explosion in 1980.

Vesuvius

The Roman city of Pompeii was buried in ash when Vesuvius erupted in AD 79. Many people who lived in Pompeii were killed.

This man covered his face to protect himself from the falling ash.

These figures are plaster casts of the bodies of people who died in Pompeii.

127

A tsunami ("soo-naa-mee").

Types of rock

Rocks come in many different colours and patterns. There are three main types of rock, shown here. They are named after the way they are made.

Igneous rocks are made when hot, melted rock called magma turns solid.

Metamorphic rocks have been heated up and changed deep underground.

Sedimentary rocks are made from layers of sand, mud, or sea creatures.

Sandstone

Sandstone is a sedimentary rock. It is made when layers of sand get squashed tightly together, over time, on the sea bed. Uluru (also called Ayers Rock) in Australia is a gigantic lump of sandstone.

Rocks and Fossils

Rocks make up the solid outer skin of the Earth – the crust. Rocks are normally hidden underground, but you can see them in mountains and at the seaside.

The Giant's Causeway

These strange rocks in Ireland are called the Giant's Causeway. They are made of an igneous rock called basalt. The rock cracked apart to form these shapes as it cooled down.

The Giant's Causeway is made up of thousands of columns of basalt rock

The wind and rain are slowly

There are many caves around the bottom of Uluru.

What is the name for a person who studies rocks?

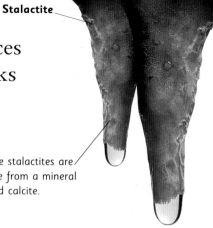

Minerals

Rocks are made up of substances called minerals. Different rocks are made up of different mixtures of minerals.

This mineral is called agate. It always has stripes of colour.

These stalactites are made from a mineral called calcite.

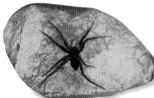

Ammonite fossil

Fossilized spider

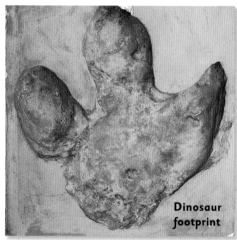

Fossils

Fossils are the bodies of plants and animals that lived millions of years ago. When they died, their bodies were buried and slowly turned to rock.

Trilobite fossil

Dinosaur footprint

Footprints in rock

Footprints left in the ground by animals millions of years ago often became fossils, too.

wearing away the rock.

The top of Uluru is 348 m (1,140 ft) above the ground.

A geologist.

Earth's materials

The Earth's rocks and minerals contain many useful materials, such as metals and gems. We also get fuels such as coal and oil from the Earth.

Hot, liquid aluminium being poured into a mould

This digger is scooping up iron ore at a mine in Brazil.

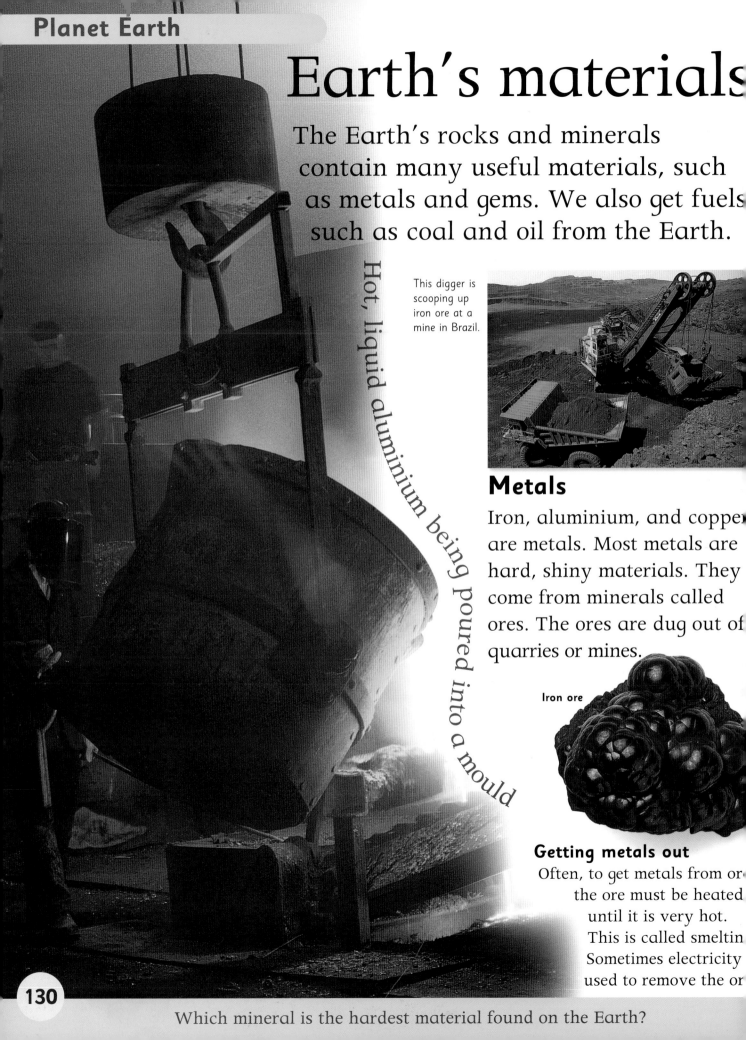

Metals

Iron, aluminium, and copper are metals. Most metals are hard, shiny materials. They come from minerals called ores. The ores are dug out of quarries or mines.

Iron ore

Getting metals out

Often, to get metals from ore, the ore must be heated until it is very hot. This is called smelting. Sometimes electricity is used to remove the ore.

Which mineral is the hardest material found on the Earth?

Gems

Some minerals found in rocks look like beautiful pieces of coloured glass. They are called gems. Sapphire, ruby, and diamond are all gems.

A diamond in the rock where it was found

A fully cut diamond

utting diamonds is very skilled job.

Using metals

Metals are good materials for making things. Here are four common metals and how we use them.

Iron has been used to make tools and weapons for thousands of years.

Copper is a brown metal. Electricity cables and coins are made of copper.

Aluminium is a lightweight metal. It is rolled thin to make kitchen foil.

Gold always stays very shiny, so we make jewellery and ornaments from it.

Become an expert

A ruby laser beam

Using gems

Gems for jewellery are carefully cut and polished to make them sparkle. Other gems are useful in industry. Rubies make laser light, and tough diamonds are used in drills.

A cut ruby

Coal mining

Coal is made from ancient plants that lived millions of years ago. It is a fuel for power stations and houses. Coal is found in thick layers underground.

Coal miners work deep underground, digging out coal.

Diamond.

Air and Atmosphere

You cannot see, touch, or smell air, but it is all around you. There is a thick layer of air all over the Earth. It is called the Earth's atmosphere.

Why we need air

Without the air, plants and animals could not live on Earth. Air contains gases that animals need to breathe and plants use to make food.

Air gets bigger

When air gets warmer, it gets bigger and takes up more space. This makes it rise upwards.

A hot-air balloon floats upwards because it is full of warm air.

Gas burners in the basket heat up the air inside the balloon.

Plants use carbon dioxide from the air to make food.

Which is the lowest layer of the atmosphere?

Gases in the air

Air is made up of several different gases mixed together. We use some of these gases for special jobs.

Oxygen makes up about a fifth of the air. Nothing can burn without oxygen.

Nitrogen makes up three-quarters of the air. It is used to make fertilizers.

Helium is used to fill up balloons, which float because helium gas is lighter than air.

Carbon dioxide is used to make the bubbles in fizzy drinks.

Neon is used inside lighting tubes. The gas glows when electricity flows through it.

Earth's atmosphere

The atmosphere makes the Earth safe to live on. It keeps out harmful rays from the Sun and space. It also keeps the Earth warm.

The atmosphere stops rays from space hitting planet Earth.

This hazy blue layer is the Earth's atmosphere.

Thinning out

As you go upwards through the atmosphere, the air becomes thinner and colder – and it gets more and more difficult to breathe. Eventually, the air runs out. Then you are in space!

At the top of a mountain, the air is very thin.

Mountaineers use breathing equipment to give them extra oxygen.

Air pollution

Cars, buses, heating boilers, and factories all put poisonous gases and smoke into the air. The gases and smoke are called air pollution.

Some gases from factories cause acid rain, which can kill trees.

Water

Water is all around us. It is in rivers and seas, in the ground, and in the air. We use water from rivers and underground for drinking and washing. It comes to our homes along pipes.

Seas and oceans

The Earth's seas and oceans are full of water. The oceans cover about two-thirds of our planet's surface. That is a lot of water!

Pacific Ocean

The Pacific Ocean covers nearly half the Earth's surface.

Water is a liquid. It always flows downwards.

Water always sticks together. Small bits of water form drops.

A wave is a hump that moves across the water's surface.

Ice

When water gets very cold, it freezes and turns into ice. Ice is a solid. When ice warms up, it melts and turns back into water. Ice is lighter than water, so lumps of ice float.

Steam

When water gets very hot, it turns into steam. Steam is a gas. When steam cools down, it turns back into water. Steam from a kettle cools quickly when it leaves the spout, making a cloud of tiny water drops.

Salt water

Have you ever tasted sea water? It is very salty. People can get salt from the sea by letting sea water dry up. Water from rain or from rivers is not salty. It is called fresh water.

How much of your body is water?

The water cycle

Water travels between the oceans, the air, the land, and rivers.

Oceans: water from the oceans and the ground goes into the air.

Clouds: when damp air rises and cools, the water turns into clouds.

Rain: water falls to the ground from the clouds as rain, hail, or snow.

Streams: the rain soaks into the ground. Some rain water runs into streams.

Rivers: water from streams is carried back to the ocean in rivers.

Water and the landscape

This deep canyon was made by water flowing down the Colorado River in the USA. The water gradually wore away the rocks and carried the pieces away.

get into it

There is invisible steam in your breath. You can see it by breathing slowly on a cold mirror. The steam cools and turns into tiny drops of water.

Water for life

Plants, animals, and people need water to live. Animals have to drink water. Plants suck up water from the ground through their roots.

Elephants visit a water hole every day to drink.

Two-thirds of your body is water.

Weather

What is the weather like today? Is it sunny or cloudy, dry or rainy, baking hot or freezing cold? The weather affects what people do and wear every day. This is why we need to know about it.

Why weather happens

The weather happens as the Sun heats the air. As the air heats up, it moves around the Earth's atmosphere. The weather helps to spread the heat and cold evenly around the Earth.

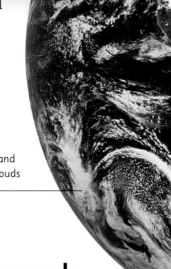

Air moves around the Earth, making wind and rain. From space, it is possible to see the clouds in the Earth's atmosphere swirling around.

Weather words

Here are some of the main features of weather. How many of them describe the weather today?

Blowing winds

Wind is air that is moving from place to place. Hurricanes bring very strong winds that blow down trees and rip the roofs off houses.

Sunshine gives us heat and light. It warms the air and dries the land.

Clouds are made from tiny water droplets. Dark clouds mean rain is on the way.

Temperature measures how hot or cold the air is, in degrees Celsius or Fahrenheit.

29°

Wind is air moving around. Winds can be light, like a breeze, or strong, like a gale.

7

Rain is drops of water that fall from clouds. Rainfall is very good for plant life.

Snow is made from tiny bits of ice. It falls instead of rain when it is very cold.

What is the name for a scientist who studies the weather?

Clouds and rain

Clouds are made up of tiny drops of water or tiny pieces (crystals) of ice. They are made when damp air rises upwards and cools. A cloudy day often means that rain or bad weather is coming.

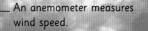
An anemometer measures wind speed.

A wind vane measures the wind direction.

Measuring weather

There are weather stations all over the world. Special instruments measure the temperature, rainfall, wind speed, and the number of hours of sunshine.

A thermometer in this box measures temperature.

Solar panel

Weather satellite

Thunder and lightning

A thunderstorm looks very dramatic. Lightning happens when electricity made inside a cloud jumps down to the ground. This makes the air heat up, which causes a loud, rumbling noise called thunder.

Forecasting the weather

Weather forecasters look at information from weather stations and pictures from weather satellites. Computers help the forecasters to work out what the weather is going to be like.

Become an expert

10-11 Deserts
14-15 Rainforests
100-101 Electricity
70-71 Plants and Food

A meteorologist.

Climate and Seasons

Climate is the type of weather a place usually has over a whole year. If the place where you live has warm summers and cool winters, it has a temperate climate.

Climate zone

Different places on Earth have different climates depending on the type of weather they get during the year.

Places near the Equator have hot, tropical climates.

Palm trees grow in tropical climates.

Tropical regions have ho weather all year round, with rain almost every da

Sub-tropical zones are also hot all year round, b have dry and rainy seaso

Desert climates are alwa dry. Deserts have hot day and freezing cold nights.

Temperate areas have warm summers and cool winters and sometimes sno

Mountain climates are cold, and often windy, with lots of rain and snow

Polar regions are very cold all the time – with ice, snow, and blizzards.

Extra-cold climates
The Arctic and Antarctic regions have very cold, polar climates. It is so cold that the sea freezes in winter!

How do desert ground squirrels stay cool?

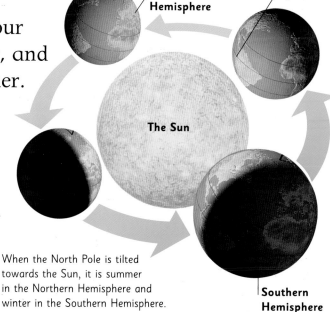

Seasons

In many places, the year is made up of four seasons. They are winter, spring, summer, and autumn. Each season has different weather.

Winter
Winter is the coldest season, with frost and snow. The days are shorter and it gets dark earlier in the evening.

Spring
In spring, the weather begins to get warmer. Trees and other plants grow leaves and flowers.

Summer
Summer is the warmest season. The days are very long, with many hours of sunshine.

Autumn
In autumn, leaves fall from the trees. Some animals hibernate, ready for winter.

Northern Hemisphere

Equator

The Sun

Southern Hemisphere

When the North Pole is tilted towards the Sun, it is summer in the Northern Hemisphere and winter in the Southern Hemisphere.

Why seasons happen

The Earth is tilted over to one side as it orbits (circles around) the Sun. As the year goes by, different places get different amounts of heat from the Sun.

Coping with climates

Animals and plants have special features that help them to live in very hot or cold climates.

Monsoon homes
Some sub-tropical places have a season of heavy rain called a monsoon. People build their houses on stilts to keep dry.

Polar bears have thick fur coats.

They use their tails as sunshades.

The Universe

The Universe contains the Sun, the Earth, other planets, everything in our galaxy, and billions of other galaxies. It also contains all the empty space in between.

A telescope from the 17th century

The first astronomers

Astronomers have studied space for thousands of years. The Italian astronomer Galileo was the first person to look at the night sky through a telescope.

Ideas about the Universe

People used to think that the Earth was at the centre of the Universe. Galileo showed that they were wrong.

We now know that the Sun is at the centre of the Solar System.

Everything in the Universe came from the Big Bang.

The Earth travels around (orbits)...

The Sun

...the Sun.

What is a black hole?

Life in space

In space, astronauts and their equipment float around because gravity does not hold them down like it does on the Earth. Astronauts have to learn how to live and work in space.

Inside spacecraft, meals are served on a special tray that stops the food floating around!

Handles and straps fixed in the floor keep the astronauts still, and help them to get around.

The Big Bang

Most astronomers think that the Universe was made more than 15 billion years ago in an enormous explosion called the Big Bang.

Modern astronomical telescope

Curiosity quiz

Look through the Space and the Universe pages to identify each of the picture clues below.

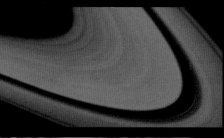

Turn and learn

24-25 World of People

64-65 World of Life

124-125 Our Planet

A place where gravity is so strong that even light cannot get out.

Stars and Galaxies

Our night sky is full of distant objects. The tiny specks of light we can see are stars, lik the Sun. A galaxy is a huge cloud of stars.

Stars

A star is a huge ball of gas that gives out light and heat. Some stars are smaller than our Sun. Some are thousands of times bigger.

New stars

Far away in space there are monster clouds of gas and dust. If the gas and dust clump together into a ball, a new star begins to shine.

A cloud of dust in space is called a nebula.

Here are the glowing remains of an old star that has died.

Old stars

Stars shine for thousands of millions of years. But they do shine for ever. When very lar stars die, they explode. The explosion is called a supernov

Which is the only galaxy we can see without a telescope?

Constellations

Thousands of years ago, people saw that the stars made shapes and patterns. They gave the patterns names. We call these star patterns constellations.

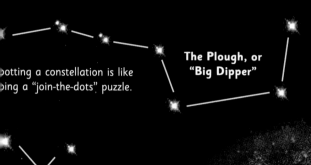

Spotting a constellation is like doing a "join-the-dots" puzzle.

The Plough, or "Big Dipper"

The Southern Cross

The Milky Way

All the stars you can see in the night sky are part of a huge star cloud called the Milky Way. This is our galaxy. It contains billions of stars.

Galaxy shapes

There are billions of galaxies in the Universe. Some are spiral shaped. Some are ball shaped. Some are not really any shape at all. The Milky Way is known as a "spiral" galaxy.

A spiral galaxy has long "arms" of stars.

The Andromeda Galaxy.

The Sun and Solar System

The Earth is part of a family of planets that move around the Sun. Together, the Sun and the planets are called the Solar System.

Planets in orbit

The planets travel around the Sun in huge, oval-shaped paths called orbits. The orbit that the Earth follows measures almost 300 million km (186 million miles) across.

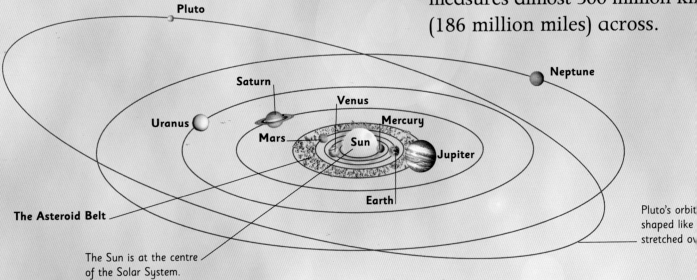

Pluto

Saturn

Venus

Uranus

Mercury

Mars

Sun

Jupiter

Neptune

Earth

The Asteroid Belt

Pluto's orbit shaped like stretched ov

The Sun is at the centre of the Solar System.

Our nearest star

The Sun is our local star. It is 150 million km (93 million miles) from Earth. It has been shining for billions of years. All the heat and light needed for life on Earth comes from the Sun.

Orbits and spins

Planets orbit the Sun at different speeds. As they orbit, they also spin around at different speeds.

Mercury is closest to the Sun. It takes just 88 days to make its orbit.

Jupiter is the biggest planet, but it spins around in less than 11 hours.

Pluto is usually furthest from the Sun. It takes 248 years to make its orbit.

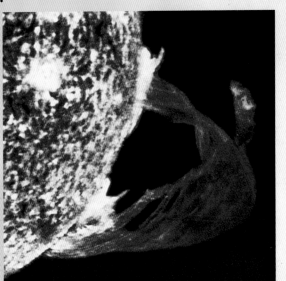

On the Sun

It is an amazing 6,000° (10,800°F) on the surfac of the Sun. Huge jets of glowing gas, called sol flares, leap up into space. Dark patches of cooler gas, called sunspots, move across the surface.

Which is the hottest planet in the Solar System?

Mercury

Venus

Earth

Gas and dust
The Sun and all the planets in the Solar System were made 4,500 million years ago from a huge cloud of gas and dust.

Mars

Planet Earth

Earth is a very special planet. It has a rocky surface, water, and an atmosphere. It is the only planet in the Solar System where animals and plants can live.

Astronomers have seen solar systems forming around other stars.

Jupiter

The Sun is 100 times wider than the Earth.

From Neptune, the Sun looks like a tiny speck of light.

Saturn

Jupiter spins so fast that its middle bulges outwards.

Neptune

Uranus

Pluto

Cold planets
Uranus, Neptune, and Pluto are billions of kilometres away from the Sun. Hardly any heat reaches them, so they are extremely cold worlds.

Venus is the hottest planet. Its thick atmosphere traps heat from the Sun.

ᴧnets and Moons

ᴧrth is a massive ball of rock moving
ᴧd the Sun. It is called a planet.
ᴧon is a ball of rock that
ᴧs around a planet.

The Moon
28 days t
the Earth.

ᴧmoon

ᴧon out tonight? The Moon is the name
ᴧo the Earth's only moon. You can see the
ᴧcause light from the Sun bounces off it.
ᴧey around planet Earth is called an orbit.

nicknamed the Red Planet.

Mars has
enormous
valleys and
mountains.

Rocky planets

The planets near the Sun ar
rocky planets. They have ᴧ
thick crust of solid rock
and hot, runny rock
inside. Mercury, Veᴧ
Earth, and Mars a
all rocky planets.

Life on other planets
This is the surface of Marᴧ
Plants and animals cannᴧ
live on Mars because therᴧ
no air and it is freezing cᴧ
But there might have beeᴧ
on Mars millions of years

What is the biggest storm on Jupiter called?

Planets with rings

Some planets have rings around them. Saturn has spectacular rings. They are made up of millions of chunks of rock and ice that orbit (circle around) Saturn.

Saturn

Saturn's rings are 20 times wider than the Earth.

Moons

There are dozens of moons in our solar system. The force of gravity keeps them travelling around their planets. This is Pluto's only moon, called Charon. It is half as big as Pluto.

Charon

Jupiter's moons

Jupiter has 16 moons. Most of them are a lot smaller than Earth's moon. These four are bigger than our moon.

Ganymede is the largest moon in the whole Solar System.

Callisto looks like our moon. It is completely covered in craters.

Io is red and yellow. It is covered in volcanoes that never stop erupting.

Europa is covered in ice. Underneath the ice there may be a huge ocean.

There are enormous, swirling storms on Jupiter.

Gas planets

Jupiter, Saturn, Uranus, and Neptune are known as the Gas Giants. These four planets, which are extremely far away from the Sun, are giant balls of gas and liquid. They do not have a solid surface like the rocky planets.

147

The Great Red Spot.

Earth's moon

The Moon is the Earth's travelling partner in space. It is a freezing cold, dusty place, where there is no air or water.

The far side of the Moon

Only astronauts have seen the far side of the Moon

The Moon's orbit

The Moon is 384,000 km (239,000 miles) away from Earth. It moves around the Earth on a journey called an orbit. Each orbit takes 28 days.

This is the view of the Moon from Earth.

The Moon does not have weather like the Earth does.

Changing shape

The Moon seems to change shape as it travels around Earth.

New Moon. This is when the Sun lights up the far side of the Moon.

Crescent Moon. Now, we can see that a tiny bit of the near side is lit up.

First quarter Moon. A few days later, we see more of the lit near side.

Gibbous Moon. Now, we can see nearly all of the lit up near side.

Full Moon. The Sun is now shining on the whole of the Moon's near side.

The near side

As the Moon moves around the Earth, it spins slowly. Because it turns exactly once every orbit, the same side always faces the Earth. We call this side the near side of the Moon.

Who was the first person to set foot on the Moon?

Visiting the Moon

So far, the Moon is the only place in the Solar System that astronauts have been to. In 1969, a mission to the Moon put two astronauts on the surface for the first time.

The service module stayed in space, above the Moon, with one astronaut – called Michael Collins – inside.

Eclipses

Sometimes, the Moon gets in the way of the Sun's light. This is called an eclipse. The Moon's shadow falls on parts of the Earth.

The lunar module landed on the Moon. Two astronauts – called Neil Armstrong and Buzz Aldrin – travelled inside it.

Craters and seas

The Moon's surface is covered in holes called craters. They were made when lumps of rock called meteorites smashed into the surface. The flat areas are known as seas.

The American astronaut Neil Armstrong.

Comets and Space rocks

Apart from the planets and moons, there are lots of bits of rock, dust, and ice floating around in the Solar System. Sometimes, we see them when they come close to Earth.

Comets

A comet is a huge lump of dust and ice hurtling through space. It is like a massive, dirty snowball. There are millions of comets in orbit around the Sun. Most of them are too far away to see.

Long tails

When a comet comes near the Sun, its ice begins to melt. This releases gas and dust into space. Rays from the Sun push the gas and dust into two long tails – a dust tail (white or yellow) and a gas tail (blue).

Comet Hale-Bopp

Asteroids look a little bit like enormous potatoes!

A comet's tail can be millions of kilometres long.

Which comet flies by Earth once every 76 years?

Meteors

Have you ever seen a shooting star (a meteor)? They happen when a small piece of dust from a comet hurtles into the Earth's atmosphere and burns up in a flash.

Big and small

Asteroids come in all sorts of sizes. Some are as small as grains of sand. The biggest one found is 920 km (572 miles) across. It is called Ceres.

Only the very biggest asteroids can be seen from Earth.

The Asteroid Belt

An asteroid is a lump of rock going around the Sun, like a tiny planet. There are millions of asteroids between Mars and Saturn. This area is called the Asteroid Belt.

Meteorites

Sometimes large lumps of rock collide with planets and moons. These are called meteorites. They crash into the surface – leaving huge, bowl-shaped holes called craters.

Mercury

Mercury's thin atmosphere does not provide much protection from meteorites.

get Mucky

Put some flour in a saucer and smooth it over. Dip your finger in water and let a drop fall into the flour. Did you get a good crater?

Many of Mercury's craters are hundreds of kilometres wide.

Halley's comet. It was named after an astronomer called Edmund Halley.

Space travel

Astronauts are people who travel into space. They do science experiments, fix satellites, and find out what living in space is like. One day, they might even travel to other planets.

The payload (cargo) that the rocket is carrying

Launch tower

The first rockets

This is Robert Goddard, an American rocket maker. In 1926, he built the first rocket that used liquid fuel. Today, most rockets that travel into space still use liquid fuel.

Rockets

Astronauts cannot get to space without a rocket. At the bottom of the rocket are very powerful motors. They send out jets of hot gas that push the rocket upwards into space.

The rocket engines start and then... Lift-off!

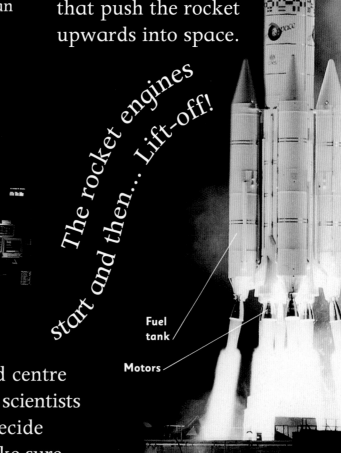

Fuel tank

Motors

Mission Control

Mission Control is a command centre on Earth. Here, engineers and scientists direct space missions. They decide when rockets take off and make sure everything is working properly.

52

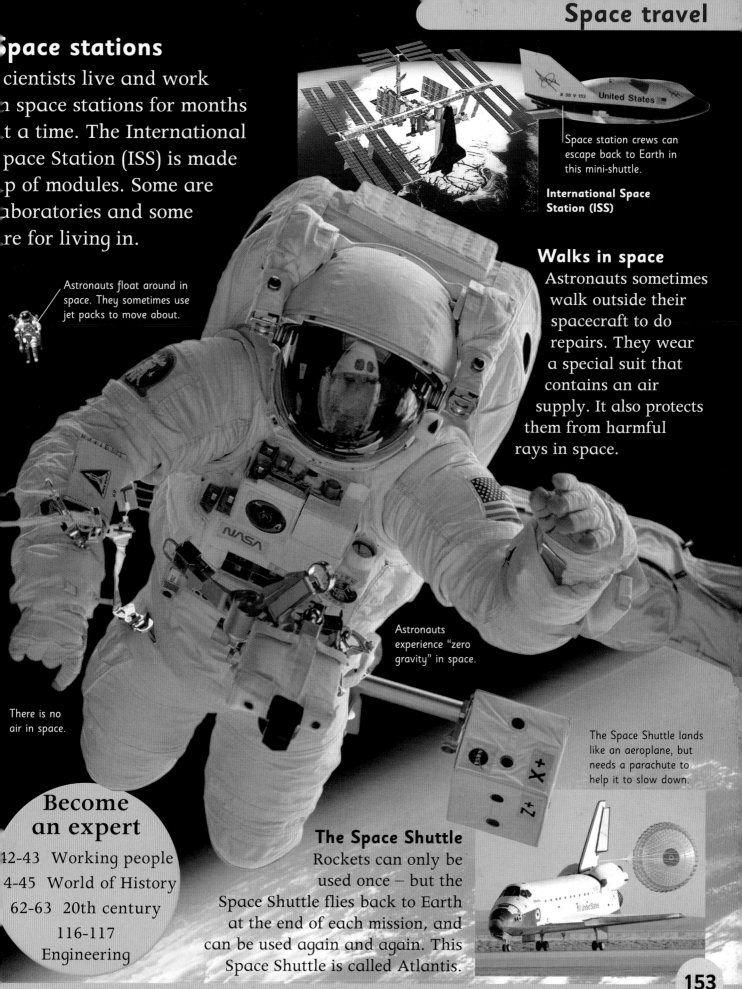

Space stations

Scientists live and work in space stations for months at a time. The International Space Station (ISS) is made up of modules. Some are laboratories and some are for living in.

Space station crews can escape back to Earth in this mini-shuttle.

International Space Station (ISS)

Astronauts float around in space. They sometimes use jet packs to move about.

Walks in space

Astronauts sometimes walk outside their spacecraft to do repairs. They wear a special suit that contains an air supply. It also protects them from harmful rays in space.

Astronauts experience "zero gravity" in space.

There is no air in space.

The Space Shuttle lands like an aeroplane, but needs a parachute to help it to slow down.

Become an expert

The Space Shuttle

Rockets can only be used once – but the Space Shuttle flies back to Earth at the end of each mission, and can be used again and again. This Space Shuttle is called Atlantis.

A dog from Russia, called Laika, in 1957.

Space exploration

Astronomers and astronauts have learnt lots of amazing things about the Universe. But there are still many things to discover.

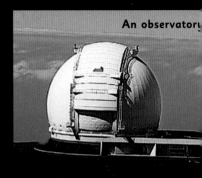

An observatory

Telescopes

Inside this dome is a large telescope. It has a huge mirror that collects light coming from space.

Telescopes make planets and stars look much bigger, helping us see these distant objects more clearly.

Radio telescopes collect rays coming from space.

A radio telescope has a huge dish that can collect lots of radio waves at once.

Radio telescopes

Some objects in space, such as black holes, cannot be seen with ordinary telescopes. Astronomers search for them using radio telescopes that can detect the invisible rays they give out.

Which space probe visited Halley's comet?

Space telescopes

Telescopes on Earth often get a blurred view of space because the Earth's atmosphere gets in the way. Telescopes floating out in space, such as the Hubble Space Telescope, give a much clearer view.

Hubble Space Telescope

This lid closes when the telescope is not being used.

Solar panels turn sunlight into electricity, which Hubble needs to work.

Man on the Moon

When astronauts visited the Moon, they did experiments and collected rocks. Their footprints, left in the dusty surface, will last for millions of years.

Space probes

Robot spacecraft are called space probes. They take photographs and use instruments to find out about planets and moons.

Luna 3 took the first photographs of the far side of the Moon in 1959.

Pioneer 10 was the first space probe to fly close to the planet Jupiter.

Venera 9 landed on the surface of Venus in 1975 and sent back photographs.

Viking 1 and **Viking 2** landed on Mars and searched for signs of life.

Voyager 1 flew past Saturn, taking photographs of its rings and moons.

Pathfinder landed on Mars with a robot vehicle that explored the surface.

Missions to Mars

One day, astronauts might visit Mars. It will take six months to get there, and six months to get back. Unmanned space probes have already been to Mars.

Robot vehicles like this one have already explored the surface of Mars.

A probe called Giotto, in 1986.

155

Website addresses

World Regions

http://www.infoplease.com/world.html...............information on countries, buildings, flags, plus an atlo

http://www.plcmc.lib.nc.us/kids/mow.........................a great website for flags and maps of the worl

http://www.countryreports.org...facts about every country in the worl

http://mbgnet.mobot.org/sets/desert/index.htm...............................find out what deserts are really lik

http://passporttoknowledge.com/rainforest/intro.html..........................your passport to the rainfores

People and Society

http://uwacadweb.uwyo.edu/religionet/er.......................learn about all the major religions of the worl

http://www.metmuseum.org/explore.......................................explore a museum full of great works of a

http://library.thinkquest.org/10098...architecture through the age

http://www.childrensmusic.org...........................everything you need to know about music for childre

http://www.sikids.com...a sports news website especially for youngster

History of People

http://www.guardians.net/egypt/kids...........the ancient Egypt "kid connection" – loads of fun activitie

http://www.pbs.org/wgbh/nova/vikings...enter the world of the Vikinc

http://www.pbs.org/wgbh/nova/peru.......................................discover the ice mummies of the Inco

http://eduscapes.com/42explore/castle.htm...................provides lots of links to websites about castle

http://www.enchantedlearning.com/explorers/indexa.shtml..........an amazing A–Z index of explorer

Use the Internet to find out more about...

...people, their culture

...world regions

...and their history

...the livi

Every effort has been made to ensure that the websites are suitable, and that their addresses a up-to-date at the time of going to print. Websi content is constantly updated, as are websi addresses – therefore, it is highly recommende that a responsible adult should visit and che each website before allowing access to a chil

Living World

http://animal.discovery.com...nothing but animals as far as the eye can see!

http://www.earthlife.net.............................this will help you to find your way around the animal kingdom

http://www.bbc.co.uk/nature/blueplanet........dive into the world's oceans and learn about their wildlife

http://dinosaurs.eb.com.........................."Discovering Dinosaurs" – make sure you visit the "activity guide"

http://www.brainpop.com/health/seeall.weml.............a fantastic (and funny) guide to the human body

Science and Technology

http://www.hhmi.org/coolscience...................."Cool Science for Curious Kids" – lots of fun science projects

http://www.exploratorium.edu........................the website of "The Exploratorium" – a museum of science

http://www.howstuffworks.com...find out how absolutely everything works

http://www.energy.ca.gov/education.........join the "Energy Quest" – lots of stories, projects, and puzzles

http://www.colormatters.com.......................learn how colour affects the brain and body, and much more

Planet Earth

http://kids.earth.nasa.gov...a NASA website that explores our planet

http://www.geography4kids.com.............................learn about the physical geography of planet Earth

http://www.crustal.ucsb.edu/ics/understanding..............loads of great information about earthquakes

http://www.rogersgroupinc.com/ourcommunities/rockology/index.htm...Rockology! Info. and games

http://www.learner.org/exhibits/weather.............................explore the forces behind the world's weather

Space and the Universe

http://kids.msfc.nasa.gov...............the official "NasaKids" website – news stories, info., and activities

http://starchild.gsfc.nasa.gov...................."StarChild" – a learning centre for young astronomers

http://library.thinkquest.org/28327.............................a "Virtual Journey into the Universe"

http://www.kidsastronomy.com.......introduce yourself to astronomy and the Solar System

http://www.dustbunny.com/afk/index.html......................more astronomy for kids!

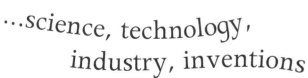

...science, technology, industry, inventions

...our amazing planet

...and other worlds.

World

Reference Section

Index

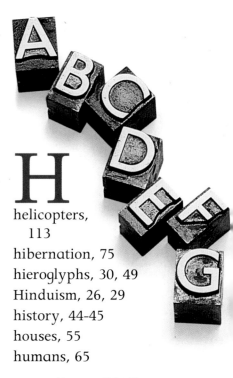

Key to measurements

Length, distance, and area
km = kilometres m = metres
cm = centimetres ft = feet in = inches
square km = square kilometres
Speed km/h = kilometres per hour
mph = miles per hour

Weight and volume kg = kilograms
g = grams lb = pounds
Temperature °C = degrees Celsius
°F = degrees Fahrenheit
Years and dates years BC (Before Christ) =
the years **before** the birth of Jesus Christ

years AD (Anno Domini – "in the year of
the Lord") = the years **since** the birth
of Jesus Christ
Very large numbers
1 million (1,000,000) = 1,000 x 1,000
1 billion (1,000,000,000) = 1,000 x 1 million

Acknowledgements

Dorling Kindersley would like to thank:

Andrew O'Brien for original graphic artworks; Chris Bernstein for compiling the index; Lisa Magloff, Amanda Rayner, and Penny York for editorial assistance and proof reading; Jacqueline Gooden, Claire Penny, Mary Sandberg, and Cheryl Telfer for design assistance; David Roberts for DK cartography; Angela Anderson and Sean Hunter for additional agency picture research; Sally Hamilton, Rose Horridge, Sarah Mills, and Charlotte Oster for DK Picture Library research; Charlie Gordon-Harris for in-house assistance; David Holland for the use of his traditional "Punch and Judy" puppets; and Victoria Waddington for photo shoot assistance.

Picture credits